THE
List Lover's
GUIDE TO
Jane Austen

JOAN STRASBAUGH

sourcebooks
casablanca

Illustrations by Janet Trembley: pages 29, 74, 76, 96, 110, 139. By courtesy of the Department
of Special Collections, Memorial Library, University of Wisconsin–Madison: 53, Chawton
Cottage, from *The Letters of Jane Austen* by Sarah Chauncey Woolsey. Jane Austen House Museum:
142. *Jane Austen's Letters in Facsimile: Reproductions of Every Known Extant Letter, Fragment, and
Autograph Copy, with an Annotated List of All Known Letters*, by Jo Modert, published by Southern
Illinois University Press: 116, 126. Page 14 HMS *Canopus*; 38 and 130, the Prince Regent from
Men, Maidens, and Manners a Hundred Years Ago, by John Ashton; 44 and 87 from *Modern Cookery*
by Eliza Acton; 62 Stoneleigh Abbey, 90 and 105 from *Jane Austen: Her Homes and Her Friends*,
by Constance Hill; 72 and 158 from *The History of Little Goody Two-Shoes*; 152 Sweet William;
164 Drury Lane Theatre; 176 *Gallery of Fashion*, London, 1795; 185 from *Persuasion*, edited by
Reginald Brimley, published by Chatto & Windus; 203 Mary Queen of Scots by Cassandra Austen
from *The History of England by Jane Austen*.

Published by Sourcebooks Casablanca, an imprint of Sourcebooks, Inc.
P.O. Box 4410, Naperville, Illinois 60567-4410
(630) 961-3900
Fax: (630) 961-2168
www.sourcebooks.com

Library of Congress Cataloging-in-Publication Data
Strasbaugh, Joan.
  The list lover's guide to Jane Austen / Joan Strasbaugh.
    pages cm
  Includes bibliographical references.
  (trade paper : alk. paper) 1. Austen, Jane, 1775-1817—Handbooks, manuals, etc. I. Title.
  PR4036.S77 2013
  823'.7—dc23
  [B]

                                    2012049873

             Printed and bound in the United States of America.
                 VP 10 9 8 7 6 5 4 3 2 1

For Ian and Ellen

Contents

Acknowledgments

A s you can imagine, many, many people and institutions contributed information for this book. My gratitude to them is immense.

But it would be impossible not to acknowledge those without whom *The List Lover's Guide to Jane Austen* would not have come to be.

TWO BIG BOOKS OF LISTS

- Deirdre Le Faye's *A Chronology of Jane Austen*
- David Gilson's *A Bibliography of Jane Austen*

TWO KEYS TO THE KINGDOM OF JANE AUSTEN

- Deirdre Le Faye's *Jane Austen's Letters* and *Jane Austen: A Family Record*

THREE REMARKABLE RESOURCES FOR FACSIMILES OF JANE AUSTEN'S MANUSCRIPTS

- *Jane Austen's Letters in Facsimile: Reproductions of Every Known Extant Letter, Fragment, and Autograph Copy, with an Annotated List of All Known Letters*, by Jo Modert
- Jane Austen's Fiction Manuscripts Digital Edition, janeausten.ac.uk
- The Morgan Library, themorgan.org

SEARCHTASTIC WEBSITES

- The Republic of Pemberley, pemberley.com
- Project Gutenberg, gutenberg.org
- JaneAustensFamily.co.uk

PEOPLE AND PLACES HELPING
IN THE HUNT FOR INFO

- British Library
- British Museum
- Jeanice Brooks
- Ronald Dunning
- Susannah Fullerton
- Ian Gammie
- David Gilson
- Hampshire Museums Service

- Deirdre Le Faye
- Lyme Regis Museum
- David Selwyn
- Isabel Snowden, Jane Austen's House
- Sotheby's
- Southern Illinois University Press

LIBRARIES!

- Madison Public Library
- Morgan Library and Museum
- New York Public Library
- University of California Libraries

- University of Chicago Library
- Susan Stravinski, Department of Special Collections, University of Wisconsin–Madison Libraries

JANEITES EXTRAORDINAIRE

- Kathy Egstad
- Cheryl Kinney
- Arnie Perlstein

- Jane Austen Society of North America
- Mary Williams

CAN'T THANK YOU ENOUGH FOR YOUR HELP

- Ian Armitage
- Ellen Dupont
- Mary Feeney

- Rosalie Robertson
- Jeff Stone
- Janet Trembley

AS ALWAYS

- My sister Kathy Strasbaugh
- My dear friend Martha Andrew

- Andrew Davies, who got the Jane Austen ball rolling

And a huge thank you to the hardworking people at Sourcebooks who made it all happen.

Foreword

One of the most endearing things about Emma Woodhouse is her propensity to make lists. We know Mr. Knightley mentions the lists Emma makes of all the books she means to read, but I suspect that Emma has other lists—in her bedroom, tucked into books, or left scattered around Hartfield. They are lists of those whose portraits she intends to draw, lists of new furnishings she would like to gradually introduce into Hartfield, lists of games to play with her nephews next time they visit, and lists of things she must remember NOT to mention in front of her father. And other Jane Austen characters probably have their share of lists, too. As an ardent list-maker myself, I like to picture Jane Austen's characters with similar addictions, even if, like Emma, they never get around to actually crossing things off their lists.

There is no better way of recommending this book than to make a list, so...

TEN REASONS FOR READING THIS BOOK

1. You will find it an extremely useful reference guide. Next time you need to check how many characters are clergymen, or which books Jane Austen is known to have read, or where her homes were, or how each of her books begins and ends, you can turn to this book.
2. It will help you win those Jane Austen trivia quizzes which pop up so often.

3. It will teach you new things about Jane Austen's life—we tend to think of her life as a very quiet and confined one, but just look at the list of people she knew and mentions in her letters.

4. It will teach you new things about Jane Austen's characters—just how many of them there are in each novel, what books they quote from, what they look like, what their professions are, and how they can sometimes be summarized by one quote.

5. It will teach you about the era in which Jane Austen lived—what wars took place and who ruled England during her lifetime.

6. It provides helpful timelines for all her novels—dates started and completed, publication dates, etc., as well as useful lists of her poetry.

7. It lists all the locations, real and imagined, where Jane Austen places her characters.

8. It includes many delightful quotes, reminding you all over again why Jane Austen is the greatest novelist of all time (for, in my list, she is!).

9. Some lists will surprise and intrigue you with their groupings of facts not often collected in this way.

10. It will entertain you!

—Susannah Fullerton
President of the Jane Austen Society of Australia
Author of *Jane Austen and Crime*, *A Dance with Jane Austen:
How a Novelist and Her Characters Went to the Ball*, and
Happily Ever After: Celebrating Jane Austen's Pride and Prejudice

Note about the Text

In an attempt to be true to Jane Austen's original work, we used the earliest versions of her letters and novels. Capitalizations and misspellings, for instance, were in her handwriting. For her letters, Deirdre Le Faye's *Jane Austen's Letters*, Fourth Edition, is our guide. For her novels, we used the *Oxford Illustrated Jane Austen*.

Introduction

What do we actually know about Jane Austen? What are the facts? And wouldn't it be fun to write them all down? That's how this book began: with a love of Jane Austen and a need to make neat little (!) lists.

- Where exactly did she live?
- How many siblings did she have?
- Who were her best friends?
- What did she do for fun?
- Who were her heartthrobs?
- All the first lines of her novels
- What she read
- What she wore
- What about her stuff?
- &c, &c, as Jane would say

In this book, we'll highlight all the people and places of Jane's lifetime. Just the facts—nieces and nephews born after she died are not listed, and places her friends or family *may* have traveled (but there's no evidence she did) are not included. It all makes for a true picture of Jane's life—her letters and friends' and relatives' firsthand accounts are chock-full of fascinating tidbits—as do artifacts and reminiscences from neighbors and people who crossed her path.

As many before have discovered, trying to pin down Jane Austen is difficult—but not unexciting. We know quite a bit about her life and work, thanks to remarkable research done by scholars and enthusiasts almost from the moment she died. And new information pops up regularly, sending a rumble through the landscape, changing our "truth" just a bit. No matter. We're relentless, we're Janeites, and we're true fans.

Back to the "little" part of the lists. The biggest surprise in putting this book together was discovering the sheer number of social contacts, places visited, and characters in her books. Her social circle was enormous and her travels many, mirrored in her novels by the sixty plus characters and forty plus locations in *Sense and Sensibility*, for starters.

Do life and work connect in the world of Jane Austen? Maybe you'll find some clues here. And who knows, maybe someday *you'll* unearth an undiscovered diary. Much is left to explore, so let's begin!

JANE AUSTEN'S NOVELS

- *Sense and Sensibility*
- *Pride and Prejudice*
- *Mansfield Park*
- *Emma*
- *Northanger Abbey*
- *Persuasion*

JANE AUSTEN'S HEROINES

- Elinor Dashwood
- Marianne Dashwood
- Elizabeth Bennet
- Fanny Price
- Emma Woodhouse
- Catherine Morland
- Anne Elliot

Her Life

- Born Saturday, December 16, 1775, Steventon, Hampshire, England
- Seventh child of George and Cassandra Austen
- Seven siblings
- Lived in five locations
- Wrote six novels
- Died at age 41, 4:30 a.m. Friday, July 18, 1817, College Street, Winchester, Hampshire
- Buried Thursday, July 24, 1817, Winchester Cathedral

APPEARANCE

CONSENSUS OPINION

- Curly brown hair
- Brown or hazel eyes
- Tall and slender
- Good posture
- Tidy

PORTRAITS

Both by sister Cassandra

- A watercolor of Jane seated outdoors, her face concealed by a big blue bonnet. Signed "C.E.A. 1804." The painting is privately owned.

"A sketch which Aunt Cassandra made of her in one of their expeditions—sitting down out of doors on a hot day, with her bonnet strings untied."

—niece Anna Lefroy

- An unfinished watercolor of Jane, circa 1810, posing with her arms crossed and a not happy expression on her face. On display in the National Portrait Gallery, London.

"Hideously unlike"

—niece Cassy Esten Austen

"I did not reckon upon finding any likeness—but there is a look which I recognise as hers—and though the general resemblance is not strong, yet as it represents a pleasant countenance it is so far a truth—& I am not dissatisfied with it."

—niece Caroline Austen

DESCRIPTIONS OF HER APPEARANCE AND PERSONALITY DURING HER LIFETIME

"The youngest [Jane] is very like her brother Henry, not at all pretty & very prim, unlike a girl of twelve: but it is hasty judgement which you will scold me for… Jane is whimsical & affected."

—COUSIN PHILADELPHIA (PHYLLY) WALTER, JULY 23, 1788

"I hear her Sister & herself are two of the prettiest Girls in England."

—COUSIN ELIZA DE FEUILLIDE, SUMMER 1791

"Cassandra & Jane are both very much grown (The latter is now taller than myself) and greatly improved as well in Manners as in Person both of which are now much more formed than when You saw them, They are I think equally sensible, and both so to a degree seldom met with, but still My Heart gives the preference to Jane, whose kind partiality to me, indeed requires a return of the same nature."

—ELIZA DE FEUILLIDE, AUGUST 1792

DESCRIPTIONS FROM MEMORY

"The Figure tall & slight, but not drooping; well balanced, as was proved by her quick firm step—Her complexion of that rather rare sort which seems the peculiar property of <u>light brunettes</u>—A mottled skin, not fair, but perfectly clear & healthy in hue: the fine naturally curling hair, neither light nor dark; the bright hazel eyes to match, & the rather small but well-shaped nose. One hardly understands how with all these advantages she could yet fail of being a decidedly handsome woman."

—ANNA LEFROY

"Her stature was that of true elegance. It could not have been increased without exceeding the middle height. Her carriage and deportment were quiet, yet graceful. Her features were separately good. Their assemblage produced an unrivalled expression of that cheerfulness, sensibility, and benevolence, which were her real characteristics. Her complexion was of the finest texture. It might with truth be said, that her eloquent blood spoke through her modest cheek."

—BROTHER HENRY AUSTEN IN PREFACE TO *NORTHANGER ABBEY*

"Mamma says she was then the prettiest, silliest, most affected, husband-hunting butterfly she ever remembered."

—FORMER NEIGHBOR MARY RUSSELL MITFORD

"Her voice was extremely sweet. She delivered herself with fluency and precision. Indeed she was formed for elegant and rational society, excelling in conversation as much as in composition. In the present age it is hazardous to mention accomplishments. Our authoress would, probably, have been inferior to few in such acquirements, had she not been so superior to most in higher things. She had not only an excellent taste for drawing, but, in her earlier days, evinced great power of hand in the management of the pencil. Her own musical attainments she held very cheap."

—HENRY AUSTEN

"Her unusually quick sense of the ridiculous led her to play with all the common-places of everyday life, whether as regarded persons or things; but she never played with its serious duties or responsibilities, nor did she ever turn individuals into ridicule. With all her neighbours in the village she was on friendly, though not on intimate, terms."

—ANNA LEFROY

"She has stiffened into the most perpendicular, precise, taciturn piece of 'single blessedness' that ever existed and that till Pride and Prejudice *showed what a precious gem was hidden in that unbending case, she was no more regarded in society than a poker or a fire screen or any other thin, upright piece of wood or iron that fills its corner in peace and quiet. The case is very different now; she is still a poker, but a poker of whom everyone is afraid."*

—FRIEND OF MARY RUSSELL MITFORD WHO WAS
INVOLVED IN A LAWSUIT WITH EDWARD KNIGHT

"When I knew Jane Austen I never suspected that she was an authoress; but my eyes told me that she was fair and handsome, slight and elegant, but with cheeks a little too full."

—STEVENTON NEIGHBOR EGERTON BRYDGES

"She was pretty—certainly pretty—bright & a good deal of color in her face—like a doll—no that wd. not give at all the idea for she had so much expression—she was like a child—quite a child very lively & full of humor—most amiable—most beloved—he says the Austins are all clever—clever in a way— they write verses &c rather elegantly & are agreeable—but not superior—that Jane & James rose far above the others & were truly superior—the others had much vanity—there was not a glimpse about those 2."

—MRS. MOZLEY'S ACCOUNT OF STEVENTON NEIGHBOR
FULWAR WILLIAM FOWLE'S RECOLLECTIONS

"As to my aunt's personal appearance, her's was the first face I can remember thinking pretty, not that I <u>used</u> that word to myself, but I know I looked at her with admiration—Her face was rather <u>round</u> than long—she had a <u>bright</u>, but not a <u>pink</u> colour—a clear brown complexion, and very good hazle eyes—She was not, I beleive, an absolute beauty, but before she left Steventon she was

established as a very pretty girl, in the opinion of most of her neighbours—as I learnt afterwards from some of those who still remained—Her hair, a darkish brown, curled naturally—it was in short curls round her face (for <u>then</u> ringlets were not). She always wore a cap—Such was the custom with ladies who were not quite young—at least of a morning but I never saw her without one, to the best of my remembrance, either morning or evening. I beleive my two Aunts were not accounted very good dressers, and were thought to have taken the garb of middle age unnecessarily soon—but they were particularly neat, and they held all untidy ways in great disesteem."

—CAROLINE AUSTEN

"I have intimated that of the two Sisters Aunt Jane was generally the favourite with children, but with the young people of Godmersham it was not so. They liked her indeed as a playfellow, & as a teller of stories, but they were not really fond of her. I believe that their Mother was not; at least that she very much preferred the elder Sister. A little talent went a long way with the Goodneston Bridgeses of that period; & <u>much</u> must have gone a long way too far."

—ANNA LEFROY

"I remember her as a tall thin <u>spare</u> person, with very high cheek bones great colour—sparkling Eyes not large but joyous & intelligent…her keen sense of humor I quite remember, it oozed out very much in Mr. Bennett's Style."

—CHAWTON NEIGHBOR CHARLOTTE MARIA MIDDLETON

"In her temper, she was chearful and not easily irritated, and tho' rather reserved to strangers so as to have been by some accused of haughtiness of manner, yet in the company of those she loved the native benevolence of her heart and kindness of her disposition were forcibly displayed."

—BROTHER FRANK AUSTEN

"I remember that when Aunt Jane came to us at Godmersham she used to bring the MS. of whatever novel she was writing with her, and would shut herself up with my elder sisters in one of the bedrooms to read them aloud. I and the younger ones used to hear peals of laughter through the door, and thought it very hard that we should be shut out from what was so delightful. I also remember how Aunt Jane would sit quietly working beside the fire in the library, saying nothing for a good while, and then would suddenly burst out laughing, jump up and run across the room to a table where pens and paper were lying, write something down, and then come back to the fire and go on quietly working as before."

—NIECE MARIANNE KNIGHT

"She had large dark eyes and a brilliant complexion, and long, long, black hair down to her knees. She was very absent indeed. She would sit silent awhile, then rub her hands, laugh to herself and run up to her room. The impression her books give one, is that she herself must have been so perfectly charming."

—LADY CAMPBELL'S VERSION OF NIECE LOUISA KNIGHT'S
(LADY GEORGE HILL'S) COMMENTS ON HER AUNT JANE

"Anne Elliot was herself; her enthusiasm for the navy, and her perfect unselfishness, reflect her completely."

—CHAWTON NEIGHBOR MRS. ANN BARRETT

"Yes my love it is very true that Aunt Jane from various circumstances was not so refined as she ought to have been from her talent & if she had lived 50 years later she would have been in many respects more suitable to our more refined tastes. They were not rich & the people around with whom they chiefly mixed, were not at all high bred, or in short anything more than mediocre & they of course tho' superior in mental powers & cultivation were on the same level as

far as <u>refinement goes</u>—but I think in later life their intercourse with Mrs. Knight (who was very fond of & kind to them) improved them both & Aunt Jane was too clever not to put aside all possible signs of 'common-ness' (if such an expression is allowable) & teach herself to be more <u>refined,</u> at least in intercourse with people in general. Both the Aunts [Cassandra & Jane] were brought up in the most complete ignorance of the World & its ways (I mean as to fashion &c) & if it had not been for Papa's marriage which brought them into Kent, & the kindness of Mrs. Knight, who used often to have one or other of the sisters staying with her, they would have been, tho' not less clever and agreeable in themselves, very much below par as to good Society and its ways. If you hate all this I beg yr. pardon, but I felt it at my <u>pen's end</u> & it chose to come along & speak the truth."

—NIECE FANNY KNIGHT KNATCHBULL IN 1869, IN
HER SEVENTIES, WRITING TO HER SISTER MARIANNE

FAMILY MEMBERS IN HER LIFETIME

"The whole World is in a conspiracy to enrich one part of our family at the expence of another."

—JANE TO CASSANDRA, MAY 21, 1801

PARENTS
Married April 26, 1764, Walcot, Bath

GEORGE AUSTEN
* May 1, 1731–January 21, 1805
* Rector of Steventon and Deane, Hampshire

+ Ran a boarding school for boys in the Austen home in Steventon

"My father reads Cowper to us in the evening, to which I listen when I can."

—JANE IN A LETTER TO HER SISTER, CASSANDRA, DECEMBER 18, 1798

CASSANDRA (LEIGH) AUSTEN

+ September 1739–January 18, 1827
+ Clergyman's daughter, born into an aristocratic family
+ She loved to garden

"My mother continues hearty; her appetite & nights are very good, but her Bowels are still not entirely settled, & she sometimes complains of an Asthma, a Dropsy, Water in her Chest & a Liver Disorder."

—JANE IN A LETTER TO CASSANDRA, DECEMBER 18, 1798

BROTHERS

JAMES AUSTEN

+ February 13, 1765–December 13, 1819
+ Attended Oxford at the age of fourteen
+ Ordained as a clergyman, 1787
+ Married twice: first to Anne Mathew, then to Mary Lloyd; three children

"I wish I had James's verses, but they were left at Chawton."

—JANE TO CASSANDRA, FROM LONDON, APRIL 20, 1811

GEORGE AUSTEN

* August 26, 1766–January 17, 1838
* Boarded with the Culham family in the neighboring village of Monk Sherborne, Hampshire, most of his life due to a disability
* No mention of him is included in Jane's surviving letters

"We have this comfort, he cannot be a bad or wicked child."

—MR. AUSTEN, JULY 8, 1770

EDWARD AUSTEN KNIGHT

* October 7, 1767–November 19, 1852
* Adopted by Mr. and Mrs. Thomas Knight II of Godmersham, 1783
* Landowner
* Married Elizabeth Bridges December 1791; eleven children

"I am tolerably glad to hear that Edward's income is so good a one—as glad as I can at anybody's being rich besides You & me—& I am thoroughly rejoiced to hear of his present to you."

—JANE TO CASSANDRA, JANUARY 8, 1799

HENRY THOMAS AUSTEN

* June 8, 1771–March 12, 1850
* Officer in the militia, banker, then clergyman; Jane's business representative in London
* Married twice; no children

* Married cousin Eliza de Feullide, December 1797
* Married Eleanor Jackson, April 1820

"Henry, who had been confined the whole day to the Bank, took me in his way home; & after putting Life & Wit into the party for a quarter of an hour, put himself & his Sister into a Hackney coach."

—JANE TO CASSANDRA, APRIL 18, 1811

FRANCIS (FRANK) WILLIAM AUSTEN

* April 23, 1774–August 10, 1865
* Entered the Royal Naval Academy at age eleven; ended his career as an admiral
* Married twice
* Married Mary Gibson in July 1806; eleven children
* Married Martha Lloyd, Jane's dear friend, July 1828; no children

"If you don't buy a muslin Gown now on the strength of this Money, & Frank's promotion, I shall never forgive You."

—JANE TO CASSANDRA, DECEMBER 28, 1798

CHARLES AUSTEN

+ June 23, 1779–October 7, 1852
+ Educated at the Royal Naval Academy at age twelve; ended career as a rear admiral
+ Married Frances Fitzwilliam Palmer, May 1807, who died on a ship; four daughters
+ Married her sister Harriet Ebel Palmer, August 1820; four children

"This said Capt. Simpson told us, on the authority of some other Captn just arrived from Halifax, that Charles was bringing the Cleopatra home, & that she was probably by this time in the Channel—but, as Capt. S. was certainly in liquor, we must not quite depend on it."

—JANE TO CASSANDRA, APRIL 25, 1811

SISTER

CASSANDRA ELIZABETH AUSTEN

+ January 9, 1773–March 22, 1845
+ Jane's closest companion
+ Engaged to Tom Fowle, who died of yellow fever in Santo Domingo, West Indies, February 1797

"May the Almighty sustain you all—& keep you, my dearest Cassandra well—but for the present I dare say you are equal to everything."

—JANE TO CASSANDRA, OCTOBER 13, 1808

AUNTS

PHILADELPHIA HANCOCK

- 1730–1792
- George Austen's sister
- Went to India to find a husband and six months later married East India Company surgeon Tysoe Saul Hancock in 1753; one daughter, Eliza

LEONORA AUSTEN

- 1732–1783
- Never married, lodged with booksellers' families in London
- Supported by her brother and sister

JANE LEIGH COOPER

- 1736–1783
- Married Dr. Edward Cooper; two children, Edward and Jane
- Probably died of typhus caught at the school where her daughter and nieces Jane and Cassandra were boarding in Southampton

UNCLES

JAMES LEIGH-PERROT

- 1735–1817
- Married heiress Jane Cholmeley in 1764; no children
- Lived in Bath some of the time and hosted the Austen family

* Mrs. Leigh-Perrot charged in 1799, then acquitted, of shoplifting lace, but not before serving time at the Somerset County Gaol in Ilchester

"My Uncle & Aunt have been with us, & shew us every imaginable kindness."
—Jane to Cassandra, January 21, 1805

Thomas Leigh

* 1747–1821
* Cared for by other families, including the Culhams of Monk Sherborne, like George Austen Jr.

William Hampson Walter

* 1721–1798
* Half brother of Jane's father
* Married Susannah Weaver; eight children

COUSINS

Elizabeth (Eliza) Hancock de Feuillide, later Austen

* 1761–1813
* Married Jean-Francois Capot (Comte) de Feuillide, captain in the Queen's Regiment of Dragoons, who was guillotined in Paris in 1794; one son, Hastings, who died young
* Her second husband was cousin Henry Austen, Jane's brother; no children

"She has plenty of business on her hands just now—for the day of the Party is settled, & drawing near;—above 80 people are invited for next tuesday Eveng & there is to be some very good Music, 5 professionals, 3 of them Glee-singers, besides Amateurs."

—JANE TO CASSANDRA, APRIL 18, 1811

JAMES WALTER

- 1759–1845
- Married distant cousin Frances Maria Walter; eighteen children

PHILADELPHIA (PHYLLY) WALTER

- 1761–1834
- Married George Whitaker; no children

"Your Christmas Gaieties are really quite surprising; I think they would satisfy even Miss Walter herself."

—JANE TO CASSANDRA, JANUARY 3, 1801

EDWARD COOPER

- 1770–1833
- Clergyman, hymn composer, and published writer of sermons
- Married Caroline Isabella Powys in 1793; eight children

"We do not much like Mr. Cooper's new Sermons;—they are fuller of Regeneration & Conversion than ever—with the addition of his zeal in the cause of the Bible Society."

—JANE TO CASSANDRA, SEPTEMBER 9, 1816

JANE COOPER (LADY WILLIAMS)

+ 1771–1798
+ Married in 1792 to Captain Thomas Williams; no children
+ Killed while driving herself through Newport, Isle of Wight, when a runaway horse crashed into her carriage

"Our first cousins seem all dropping off very fast. One is incorporated into the family [Eliza de Feuillide] another dies [Lady Williams], and a third [Edward Cooper] goes into Staffordshire."

—JANE TO CASSANDRA, JANUARY 21, 1799

NIECES

JAMES AUSTEN'S DAUGHTERS

JANE ANNA ELIZABETH AUSTEN (ANNA LEFROY)

+ 1793–1872
+ Wrote stories that she shared with her Aunt Jane; saved her letters
+ Married Benjamin Lefroy in 1814

"Anna will not be surprised that the cutting off her hair is very much regretted by several of the party in this house; I am tolerably reconciled to it by considering that two or three years may restore it again."

—JANE TO CASSANDRA, JUNE 17, 1808

CAROLINE MARY CRAVEN AUSTEN

+ 1805–1880
+ Wrote stories she shared with Jane as well as a memoir, *My Aunt Jane: A Memoir*, in 1867, about her aunt

"I look forward to the 4 new Chapters with pleasure.—But how can you like Frederick better than Edgar?—You have some eccentric Tastes however I know, as to Heroes & Heroines."

—JANE TO CAROLINE AUSTEN, FEBRUARY 26, 1817

EDWARD KNIGHT'S DAUGHTERS

FANNY CATHERINE KNIGHT

+ 1793–1882
+ Confided in her aunt on affairs of the heart; kept their correspondence
+ Married Sir Edward Knatchbull in 1820; nine children, one of them Lord Brabourne, who edited the *Letters of Jane Austen* in 1884

"Anything is to be preferred or endured rather than marrying without Affection; and if his deficiencies of Manner &c &c strike you more than all his good qualities, if you continue to think strongly of them, give him up at once."

—JANE TO FANNY, NOVEMBER 18, 1814

ELIZABETH (LIZZY) KNIGHT

+ 1800–1884
+ Married Edward Royd Rice, 1818; fifteen children

"Lizzy's work is charmingly done. Shall you put it to your Chintz?"

—JANE TO CASSANDRA, NOVEMBER 24, 1815

MARIANNE KNIGHT

+ 1801–1896
+ Lived at Godmersham until her father died in 1852, then with her brother Brook John and then her niece in Ireland

"& pray let Marianne know, in private, that I think she is quite right to work a rug for Uncle John's Coffee urn, & that I am sure it must give great pleasure to herself now, & to him when he receives it."

—JANE TO CASSANDRA, JANUARY 10, 1809

LOUISA KNIGHT

+ 1804–1889
+ Jane Austen's goddaughter
+ Married Lord George Augusta Hill in Denmark in 1847 after his first wife, Louisa's younger sister Cassandra, died; one son

CASSANDRA JANE KNIGHT

+ 1806–1842
+ Married Lord George Augusta Hill; four children

"Elizabeth, who was dressing when we arrived, came to me for a minute attended by Marianne, Charles, and Louisa, and, you will not doubt, gave me a very affectionate welcome. That I had received such from Edward also I need not mention; but I do, you see, because it is a pleasure. I never saw him look in better health, and Fanny says he is perfectly well. I cannot praise Elizabeth's looks, but they are probably affected by a cold. Her little namesake has gained in beauty in the last three years, though not all that Marianne has lost. Charles is not quite so lovely as he was. Louisa is much as I expected, and Cassandra I find handsomer

than I expected, though at present disguised by such a violent breaking-out that she does not come down after dinner. She has charming eyes and a nice open countenance, and seems likely to be very lovable. Her size is magnificent."

—JANE TO CASSANDRA, JUNE 15, 1808

FRANK AUSTEN'S DAUGHTERS

MARY JANE AUSTEN

+ 1807–1836
+ Married Royal Navy Commander George Thomas Maitland Purvis

"Her features are as delicate as Mary Jane's, with nice dark eyes, & if she had Mary Jane's fine colour, she wd be quite complete."

—JANE TO CASSANDRA, JUNE 20, 1808

CASSANDRA ELIZA AUSTEN

+ 1814–1849

"Now, little Cass & her attendant are travelling down to Chawton;—I wish the day were brighter for them. If Cassy should have intended to take any sketches while the others dine, she will hardly be able."

—JANE TO CASSANDRA, MAY 20, 1813

ELIZABETH AUSTEN

+ 1817–1830

"Mrs. F.A. has had a much shorter confinement than I have—with a Baby to produce into the bargain."

—JANE AUSTEN TO ANNE SHARP, MAY 22, 1817

CHARLES AUSTEN'S DAUGHTERS

CASSANDRA ESTEN AUSTEN

* 1808–1897
* Executed her godmother Cassandra's will related to personal effects and took possession of some of Jane Austen's memorabilia

"Ruoy xis snisuoc emac ereh yadretsey, dna dah hcae a eceip fo ekac."

—JANE TO CASSANDRA ESTEN, JANUARY 8, 1817

HARRIET JANE AUSTEN

* 1810–1865
* One of Jane's goddaughters

"Harriet is a truely sweet-tempered little Darling."

—JANE TO CASSANDRA, JULY 3, 1813

FRANCES PALMER AUSTEN

* 1812–1882
* Married cousin Francis William Austen Jr. in 1843

"I don't think little Fanny is quite so pretty as she was; one reason is because she wears short petticoats, I believe."

—JANE TO CASSANDRA, OCTOBER 18, 1813

NEPHEWS

JAMES AUSTEN'S SON BY SECOND MARRIAGE

JAMES EDWARD AUSTEN-LEIGH

- 1798–1874
- Vicar and author
- Married Emma Smith; ten children
- Wrote *Memoir of Jane Austen* in 1869; son William and grandson Richard Arthur wrote *Jane Austen, Her Life and Letters: A Family Record* in 1913; daughter Mary Augusta wrote *Personal Aspects of Jane Austen* in 1920

"Edward is writing a Novel—we have all heard what he has written—it is extremely clever; written with great ease & spirit; if he can carry it on in the same way, it will be a firstrate work, & in a style, I think, to be popular."

—JANE TO CASSANDRA, SEPTEMBER 4, 1816

EDWARD KNIGHT'S SONS

EDWARD KNIGHT

- 1794–1879
- Married his sister Fanny's stepdaughter, Mary Dorothea Knatchbull eloping to Gretna Green, Scotland in 1826; seven children
- His second wife was Adela Portal; nine children

"Edward is no Enthusiast in the beauties of Nature. His Enthusiasm is for the Sports of the field only."

—Jane to brother Francis, September 25, 1813

George Thomas Knight

- 1795–1867
- Married Lady Nelson; no children

"I flatter myself that <u>itty Dordy</u> will not forget me at least under a week. Kiss him for me."

—Jane to Cassandra, October 24, 1798

Henry Knight

- 1797–1843
- Major in the Light Dragoons
- Married cousin Sophia Cage; one son
- Charlotte Northey was his second wife; one daughter

"Henry is generally thought very good-looking but not so handsome as Edward.—I think I prefer his face."

—Jane to Fanny Knight, February 21, 1817

William Knight

- 1798–1873
- Curate and rector of Steventon, following in the footsteps of his grandfather
- Three wives: Caroline Portal (eight children), Mary Northey (three children), and Jane Hope

"Wm & I are the best of friends. I love him very much.——Everything is so <u>natural</u> about him, his affections, his Manners & his Drollery.——He entertains & interests us extremely."

—JANE TO FANNY KNIGHT, MARCH 13, 1817

CHARLES BRIDGES KNIGHT

+ 1803–1867
+ Rector of Chawton

BROOK JOHN KNIGHT

+ 1808–1878
+ Army captain
+ Married Margaret Pearson; no children

"We are heartily rejoiced that the poor Baby gives you no particular anxiety."

—JANE TO CASSANDRA, OCTOBER 16, 1808

FRANK AUSTEN'S SONS

FRANCIS WILLIAM AUSTEN

+ 1809–1858
+ Married cousin Frances Palmer Austen; no children

My dearest Frank, I wish you Joy
Of Mary's safety with a boy,
Whose birth has given little pain,
Compared with that of Mary Jane.

—JANE IN A LETTER TO BROTHER FRANK, JULY 26, 1809

HENRY EDGAR AUSTEN

- 1811–1854
- Barrister
- Committed suicide

"I give you joy of our new nephew, & hope if he ever comes to be hanged, it will not be till we are too old to care about it."

—JANE TO CASSANDRA, APRIL 25, 1811

GEORGE AUSTEN

- 1812–1903
- Clergyman
- Married Louisa Lane Tragett; five children

"Little George could tell me where you were gone to, as well as what you were to bring him, when I asked him the other day."

—JANE TO CASSANDRA, SEPTEMBER 8, 1816

HERBERT GREY AUSTEN

- 1815–1888
- Naval captain
- Married Louisa Frances Lyns; three children

"I send my Love to little Herbert."

—JANE TO CASSANDRA, NOVEMBER 24, 1815

Where She Lived

STEVENTON, HAMPSHIRE

- Jane lived here from birth to 1801
- Population of 150 in 1798

The Rectory

- Two stories
- Valued at £300
- Red-tiled roof
- Plain brick
- Three rooms in the front on the ground floor
  - Best parlor
  - Common parlor
  - Kitchen
- Back rooms
  - Mr. Austen's study
  - Back kitchen
  - Stairs
- Upstairs
  - Seven bedrooms
  - Three attics
  - Jane's and Cassandra's drawing room
    - Blue wallpaper
    - Blue-striped curtains
    - Chocolate-colored wardrobe with bookshelves
    - Chocolate-colored carpet

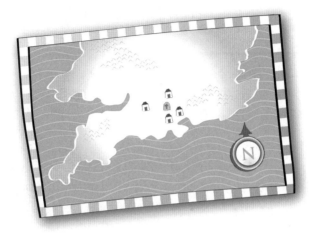

♦ Grounds

- · Enclosed garden
- · Row of spruce trees
- · Turf terrace walk
- · Small gate that led to the "Wood Walk"
- · Tall elm trees along the walk
- · Another gate that led to the church
- · Weathercock on a pole
- · Bench

JANE'S ROOM

"This room, the Dressing room, as they were pleased to call it, communicated with one of smaller size where my two Aunts slept; I remember the common-looking carpet with its chocolate ground that covered the floor, and some portions of the furniture. A painted press, with shelves above for books, that stood with its back to the wall next the Bedroom, & opposite the fireplace; my Aunt Jane's Pianoforte—& above all, on a table between the windows, above which hung a looking-glass, 2 Tonbridge-ware work boxes of oval shape, fitted up with ivory barrels containing reels for silk, yard measures, etc. I thought them beautiful & so perhaps in their day, & their degree, they were."

—ANNA LEFROY

"Our Improvements have advanced very well;—The bank along the <u>Elm Walk</u> is sloped down for the reception of Thorns and Lilacs, & it is settled that the other side of the path is to continue turf'd & be planted with Beech, Ash, & Larch."

—JANE TO CASSANDRA, OCTOBER 26, 1800

BATH

+ 1801–1806
+ Population 33,000 in 1801

4 SYDNEY PLACE

+ 1801–1804
+ £150 per year for a three and one-quarter–year lease
+ Four stories plus a basement
+ Across from Sydney Gardens, a park that included a labyrinth

"& there is a public Breakfast in Sydney Gardens every morning, so that we shall not be wholly starved."

—JANE TO CASSANDRA, MAY 17, 1799, DURING A
VISIT TO BATH WHILE STAYING AT QUEEN SQUARE

3 GREEN PARK BUILDINGS

* 1804–1805
* At the edge of Bath

Jane's opinion of these buildings when she first saw them in 1801 during initial house search: "When you arrive, we will at least have the pleasure of examining some of these putrifying Houses again;—they are so very desirable in size & situation, that there is some satisfaction in spending ten minutes within them."

—JANE TO CASSANDRA, MAY 21, 1801

25 GAY STREET

* 1805

Writing from Gay Street: "What a different set we are now moving in! But seven years I suppose are enough to change every pore of one's skin, & every feeling of one's mind.—We did not walk long in the Crescent yesterday, it was hot & not crouded enough; so we went into the field, & passed close by Stephen Terry & Miss Seymer again."

—JANE TO CASSANDRA, APRIL 8, 1805

TRIM STREET

✦ 1806

"In the meantime she assures you that she will do everything in her power to avoid Trim St altho' you have not expressed the fearful presentiment of it, which was rather expected."

—JANE TO CASSANDRA, JANUARY 3, 1801

SOUTHAMPTON

✦ 1806–1809
✦ Population 10,660 in 1801

TEMPORARY LODGINGS, LOCATION UNKNOWN

✦ October 1806–March 1807

CASTLE SQUARE

✦ March 1807–July 1809
✦ £130 rent
✦ Situated along the town's harbor wall
✦ Garden
  · Sweetbriar and roses bordered a gravel walk
  · Border under the terrace walk included syringas, laburnum, currants, gooseberries, raspberries

"We hear that we are envied our House by many people, & that the Garden is the best in the Town."

—JANE TO CASSANDRA FROM CASTLE SQUARE, FEBRUARY 22, 1807

CHAWTON

+ July 7, 1809–May 24, 1817
+ Population sixty families, four hundred inhabitants

Chawton cottage

+ Built in 1690
+ L-shaped
+ Eight rooms
+ As described by niece Caroline Austen:
  - Kitchen
  - Dining room
  - Drawing room
  - Well-furnished
  - Comfortable
  - Ladylike
  - Low ceilings
  - Roughly finished
  - Some bedrooms very small
+ Garrets
+ Dining room faces the road
+ Garden:
  - Flowers: peonies, mignonette, pinks, Sweet Williams, columbine, syringas
  - Fruit: gooseberries, apricots, Orleans plums
  - Trees: beech, yew
  - Bench
  - Outbuildings

Our Chawton home—how much we find
Already in it to our mind,
And how convinced that when complete,
It will all other Houses beat,
That ever have been made or mended,
With rooms concise or rooms distended.

—JANE TO BROTHER FRANK, JULY 26, 1809

WINCHESTER
May 24, 1817–July 18, 1817

8 COLLEGE STREET, SECOND STORY

"Our lodgings are very comfortable. We have a neat little Drawg-room with a Bow-window overlooking Dr. Gabell's Garden."

—JANE TO NEPHEW JAMES EDWARD AUSTEN FROM
COLLEGE STREET, WINCHESTER, MAY 27, 1817

HER SOCIAL CIRCLE

Jane's Comments on Her Friends and Neighbors

STEVENTON, HAMPSHIRE

Bigg and Bigg-Wither of Manydown, Wootton St.
Lawrence, Hampshire, about six miles from Steventon

· On Lovelace Bigg-Wither, father

"Poor man!—I mean Mr. Wither—his life is so useful, his character so respectable and worthy, that I really believe there was a good deal of sincerity in the general concern expressed on his account."

· On Elizabeth Bigg, daughter

"Mr H. began with Elizabeth, and afterwards danced with her again; but <u>they</u> do not know how <u>to be particular</u>."

(Elizabeth would go on to marry William Heathcote.)

· On Catherine Bigg, daughter

"And tomorrow we must think of poor Catherine."

(The next day her friend Catherine Bigg, age thirty-three, married Reverend Herbert Hill, nearly sixty.)

· On Alethea Bigg, daughter

"I do not know what Alethea's notions of Letter writing & Note writing may be, but <u>I</u> consider her as still in my Debt."

· On Harris Bigg-Wither, son (see *The Hearts She Broke*)

"Harris seems still in a poor way, from his bad habit of body; his hand bled again a little the other day, & Dr Littlehales has been with him lately."

♦ Boltons of Hackwood Park, Basingstoke, Hampshire, about nine miles from Steventon
  · Lord Bolton and Jane Mary (Powlett) Bolton and family
  · On William Bolton, son

"One of my gayest actions was sitting down two Dances in preference to having Lord Bolton's eldest son for my Partner, who danced too ill to be endured."

- Bramston family of Oakley Hall, Hampshire, about three
  miles from Steventon

"Mrs Bramston talked a good deal of nonsense, which Mr Bramston & Mr Clark seemed almost equally to enjoy."

- Chutes of the Vyne, Hampshire, about ten miles from
  Steventon
  - On William Chute

"Wm Chute called here yesterday. I wonder what he means by being so civil."

  - On Thomas Chute

"You told me some time ago that Tom Chute had had a fall from his horse, but I am waiting to know how it happened before I begin pitying him, as I cannot help suspecting it was in consequence of his taking orders; very likely as he was going to do Duty or returning from it."

- Craven family of Hampstead Marshall and Ashdown Park,
  Berkshire, about thirty miles from Steventon
  - On Lord William Craven

"She found his manners very pleasing indeed.——The little flaw of having a Mistress now living with him at Ashdown Park, seems to be the only unpleasing circumstance about him."

  - John and Catherine Craven, and children Fulwar, Charles, and
    Elizabeth, Barton Court, Kintbury, Berkshire, twenty-four miles
    from Steventon

"You are very important with your Captain Bulmore and Hotel Master, and I trust, if your trouble over-balances your dignity on the occasion, it will be amply repaid by Mrs. Craven's approbation, and a pleasant scheme to see her."

- Deanes of Monk Sherborne, Hampshire, about nine miles from Steventon
  - Mrs. Deane
  - Harriet Deane
  - Augusta Deane

"In addition to our set at the Harwoods' ball, we had the Grants, St. Johns, Lady Rivers, her three daughters and a son, Mr. and Miss Heathcote, Mrs. Lefevre, two Mr. Watkins, Mr. J. Portal, Miss Deanes, two Miss Ledgers, and a tall clergyman who came with them, whose name Mary would never have guessed."

- Debary family of Hurstbourne Tarrant, Hampshire, about fifteen miles from Steventon

"Miss Debary, Susan & Sally all in black, but without any Statues, made their appearance, & I was as civil to them as their bad breath would allow me."

- Digweeds of Steventon Manor, a few hundred feet from the Rectory
  - Mr. and Mrs. Digweed, parents
  - Mary Digweed
  - John Digweed
  - Harry Digweed
  - James Digweed
  - William Francis Digweed
  - Francis William Digweed

"We are to have Company to dinner on friday; the three Digweeds & James. We shall be a nice silent party I suppose."

- Lord and Lady Dorchester of Kempshott Park, Hampshire, about five miles from Steventon

"Mrs Lefroy has just sent me word that Lady Dortchester means to invite me to her Ball on the 8th of January, which, tho' an humble Blessing compared with what the last page records, I do not consider as any Calamity."

- Fowle family of Kintbury, Berkshire, about twenty-four miles from Steventon
  - Reverend Thomas and Jane Craven Fowle II, parents
  - Reverend Fulwar Craven and Eliza Fowle and children

"They all dine here to day. Much good may it do us all. William & Tom are much as usual; Caroline is improved in her person; I think her now really a pretty Child."

  - Reverend Tom Fowle, Cassandra's fiancé
  - William Fowle
  - Charles Fowle

- Grant family of Worting, Hampshire, about five miles from Steventon
- Harwoods of Deane, Hampshire, about two miles from Steventon
  - Mr. and Mrs. Harwood
  - John Harwood
  - Earle Harwood
  - Charles Harwood
  - Betty Anna Maria Harwood, Mr. Harwood's sister

"This morning has been made very gay to us, by visits from our two lively Neighbours Mr Holder & Mr John Harwood."

- Heathcotes of Hursley Park, Hampshire, about twenty-four miles from Steventon
  - On Harriet Heathcote

"Miss Heathcote is pretty, but not near so handsome as I expected."

- Holders, Ashe Park House, Hampshire, less than two miles from Steventon
  - William Thorpe Holder
  - James Holder

"Your unfortunate sister was betrayed last Thursday into a situation of the utmost cruelty. I arrived at Ashe Park before the Party from Deane, and was shut up in the drawing-room with Mr. Holder alone for ten minutes."

- Lefroys of Ashe Rectory, Hampshire, just north of Ashe Park, two plus miles from Steventon
  - George Lefroy and Anne (Brydges) Lefroy, "Madam Lefroy"
  - Seven children including Benjamin Lefroy, who married Jane's niece Anna.

Angelic Woman! past my power to praise
In Language meet, thy Talents, Temper, mind,
Thy solid Worth, thy captivating Grace!—
Thou friend & ornament of Humankind!—

—FROM A POEM COMMEMORATING THE DEATH OF MADAM LEFROY

- Lyfords of Basingstoke, Hampshire, about eight miles from Steventon
  - On John Lyford, the Austens' doctor, and wife, Mary Windover Lyford

"I am much obliged to you for enquiring about my ear, & am happy to say that Mr Lyford's prescription has entirely cured me. I feel it a great blessing to hear again."

  - Reverend John Lyford
  - Daughter Mary Susannah, married Reverend James Digweed
  - Charles Lyford

"I danced twice with Warren last night, and once with Mr. Charles Watkins, and, to my inexpressible astonishment, I entirely escaped John Lyford. I was forced to fight hard for it, however."

- Mathew family of Laverstoke, Hampshire, about six miles from Steventon
  - General Edward Mathew and Lady Jane Mathew
  - Anne Mathew, wife of James Austen
  - Jane Mathew
  - Brownlow Mathew
  - Penelope Mathew

"My partners were the two St. Johns, Hooper Holder—and very prodigious—Mr. Mathew, with whom I called the last, & whom I liked the best of my little stock."

* Mildmays of Shawford, Hampshire, about twenty miles from Steventon

"We dined together and went together to Worting to seek the protection of Mrs. Clarke, with whom were Lady Mildmay, her eldest son, and a Mr. and Mrs. Hoare."

* Portals, Laverstoke, Hampshire, about six miles from Steventon
  · Mr. and Mrs. William Portal
  · John Portal, brother of William
  · On Benjamin Portal, son of William

"We had a visit yesterday morning from Mr. Benjamin Portal, whose eyes are as handsome as ever."

* Portsmouths of Hurstbourne Park, Andover, Hampshire, about nine miles from Steventon
  · Lord and Lady Portsmouth

"Lord Portsmouth surpassed the rest in his attentive recollection of you, enquired more into the length of your absence, & concluded by desiring to be 'remembered to you when I wrote next.'"

* Powletts of Winslade, Hampshire, about ten miles from Steventon
  · On Charles Powlett

"Charles Powlett gave a dance on Thursday, to the great disturbance of all his neighbours, of course, who, you know, take a most lively interest in the state of his finances, and live in hopes of his being soon ruined."

· On Mrs. Powlett

"Charles Powlett has been very ill, but is getting well again;—his wife is discovered to be everything that the Neighbourhood could wish her, silly & cross as well as extravagant."

⁕ Rices of Bramling, Kent, and Ashe and Deane, Hampshire
· Henry and Sarah Rice, parents
· On Henry Rice and wife Lucy Lefroy Rice

"Rice and Lucy made love, Mat: Robinson fell asleep, James & Mrs Augusta alternately read Dr Jenner's pamphlet on the cow pox, & I bestowed my company by turns on all."

· John Rice
· Edward Rice, married Jane's niece Lizzy Knight

⁕ Mrs. Anne Russell of Basingstoke, Hampshire, about eight miles from Steventon

⁕ St. Johns of Hampshire

"We have not regaled Mary with this news. Harry St. John is in Orders, has done duty at Ashe, and performs very well."

⁕ Terrys of Dummer, Hampshire, about three miles from Steventon
· Thomas and Elizabeth Terry, thirteen children

"Our ball was chiefly made up of Jervoises and Terrys, the former of whom were apt to be vulgar, the latter to be noisy."

· On Stephen Terry

"I danced nine dances out of ten, five with Stephen Terry, T. Chute & James Digweed & four with Catherine."

BATH, SOMERSETSHIRE

⁕ Chamberlaynes

"Mr & Mrs Chamberlayne are in Bath, lodging at the Charitable Repository;—I wish the scene may suggest to Mrs C. the notion of selling her black beaver bonnet for the relief of the poor."

⁕ Evelyns

"Edward renewed his acquaintance lately with Mr Evelyn who lives in the Queen's parade & was invited to a family dinner, which I beleive at first Eliz: was rather sorry at his accepting, but yesterday Mrs Evelyn called on us & her manners were so pleasing that we liked the idea of going very much.—The Biggs would call her a nice Woman."

⁕ Mrs. Lillingstone

"We met not a creature at Mrs Lillingstone's, & yet were not so very stupid, as I expected, which I attribute to my wearing my new bonnet & being in good looks."

⁕ Winstone family
⁕ Mary Cassandra Twisleton

"I then got Mr Evelyn to talk to, & Miss Twistleton to look at; and I am proud to say that I have a very good eye at an Adultress, for tho' repeatedly assured

that another in the same party was the <u>She</u>, I fixed upon the right one from the first.——A resemblance to Mrs. Leigh was my guide. She is not so pretty as I expected; her face has the same defect of baldness as her sister's, & her features not so handsome;——she was highly rouged & looked rather quietly & contentedly silly than anything else."

+ Mr. and Mrs. Badcock

"Mrs. Badcock and two young Women were of the same party, except when Mrs Badcock thought herself obliged to leave them, to run round the room after her drunken Husband.——His avoidance, & her pursuit, with the probable intoxication of both, was an amusing scene."

+ Mr. Woodward
+ Miss Rowe

"Our acquaintance Mr Woodward, is just married to a Miss Rowe, a young lady rich in money & music."

44

- Lady Fust
- Mrs. Busby
- Mrs. Owen
- Miss Langley
- Admiral and Mrs. Stanhope

"Another stupid party last night; perhaps if larger they might be less intolerable, but there were only just enough to make one card table, with six people to look over & talk nonsense to each other. Ly Fust, Mrs Busby & a Mrs Owen sat down with my uncle to Whist within five minutes after the three old Toughs came in, & there they sat with only the exchange of Adm: Stanhope for my Uncle, till their chairs were announced."

- Miss Bond
- Mrs. Franklyn
- Maria Somerville
- The Misses Arnold

"Yesterday Evening we had a short call from two of the Miss Arnolds, who came from Chippenham on Business; they are very civil, and not too genteel, and upon hearing that we wanted a House recommended one at Chippenham."

- Mr. and Miss Edwards
- Mr. Maitland
- Mapleton family

"I spent friday evening with the Mapletons, & was obliged to submit to being pleased inspite of my inclination. We took a very charming walk from 6 to 8 up Beacon Hill, & across some fields, to the Village of Charlecombe, which is sweetly situated in a little green Valley, as a Village with such a name ought to be.—Marianne is sensible & intelligent, & even Jane considering how fair she is, is not unpleasant."

- Pickfords
- Mrs. Lysons
- Bradshaws
- Greaves

"On friday we are to have another party, & a sett of new people to you.——The Bradshaws & Greaves's, all belonging to one another; and I hope the Pickfords."

- Mr. Philips
- Miss Wood
- Dr. Gibbs
- Mr. Bowen
- Miss Seymer
- Brownes
- Duncans
- Cookes

"My morning engagement was with the Cookes, & our party consisted of George & Mary, a Mr & Miss Bendish who had been with us at the Concert, & the youngest Miss Whitby;——not Julia, we have done with her, she is very ill, but Mary; Mary Whitby's turn is actually come to be grown up & have a fine complexion & wear great square muslin shawls."

- Mr. and Miss Bendish
- Whitby family
- Mr. F. Bonham
- Miss Armstrong

"My Evening Engagement & walk was with Miss Armstrong, who had called on me the day before, & gently upbraided me in her turn with change of manners to her since she had been in Bath, or at least of late. Unlucky me! that my

notice should be of such consequence, and my Manners so bad!—She was so well-disposed, & so reasonable, that I soon forgave her, & made this engagement with her in proof of it.—She is really an agreable girl, so I think I may like her; & her great want of a companion at home, which may well make any tolerable acquaintance important to her, gives her another claim on my attention. I shall endeavour as much as possible to keep my Intimacies in their proper place, & prevent their clashing."

- Miss Blachford
- Mrs. Elliot
- Earl and Countess Roden
- Lord and Lady Leven

"When I tell you that we have been visiting a Countess this morning, you will immediately, with great justice, but no truth, guess it to be Lady Roden: No: it is Lady Leven, the mother of Ld Balgonie. On receiving a message from Lord & Lady Leven thro' the MacKays declaring their intention of waiting on us, we thought it right to go to them. I hope we have not done too much, but the friends & admirers of Charles must be attended to.—They seem very reasonable, good sort of people, very civil, & full of his praise.—We were shewn at first into an empty Drawing-room, & presently in came his Lordship, not knowing who we were, to apologise for the servant's mistake, & tell a lie himself, that Lady Leven was not within.—He is a tall, gentlemanlike looking man, with spectacles, & rather deaf;—after sitting with him ten minutes we walked away; but Lady L. coming out of the Dining parlour as we passed the door, we were obliged to attend her back to it, & pay our visit over again.—She is a stout woman, with a very handsome face."

- Mackays

SOUTHAMPTON, HAMPSHIRE

* Martha Lloyd, friend who lived with Mrs. Austen, Cassandra, and Jane in Southampton and Chawton.
* Captain Foote

"He dined with us on Friday, and I fear will not soon venture again, for the strength of our dinner was a boiled leg of mutton, underdone even for James; and Captain Foote has a particular dislike to underdone mutton; but he was so good-humoured and pleasant that I did not much mind his being starved."

* Admiral Bertie and daughter Catherine Bertie

"Our acquaintance increase too fast. He was recognised lately by Admiral Bertie, and a few days since arrived the Admiral and his daughter Catherine to wait upon us. There was nothing to like or dislike in either."

* Mr. and Mrs. Lance

"To the Berties are to be added the Lances, with whose cards we have been endowed, and whose visit Frank and I returned yesterday. They live about a mile and three-quarters from S. to the right of the new road to Portsmouth, and I believe their house is one of those which are to be seen almost anywhere among the woods on the other side of the Itchen. It is a handsome building, stands high, and in a very beautiful situation. We found only Mrs. Lance at home, and whether she boasts any offspring besides a grand pianoforte did not appear. She was civil and chatty enough, and offered to introduce us to some acquaintance in Southampton, which we gratefully declined."

* Mr. Husket
* Lord Lansdowne

"Our Dressing Table is constructing on the spot, out of a large Kitchen Table belonging to the House, for doing which we have the permission of Mr Husket, Lord Lansdown's Painter,—domestic Painter, I shd call him, for he lives in the Castle—Domestic Chaplains have given way to this more necessary office, & I suppose whenever the Walls want no touching up, he is employed about my Lady's face."

* Catherine (Kitty) Foote

"I have this instant made my present, & have the pleasure of seeing it smiled over with genuine satisfaction. I am sure I may on this occasion call Kitty Foote, as Hastings did H. Egerton, my 'very valuable Friend.'"

* Miss Jackson
* Mr. Gunthorpe

"Miss Jackson is married to young Mr Gunthorpe, & is to be very unhappy. He swears, drinks, is cross, jealous, selfish, and Brutal.—the match makes <u>her</u> family miserable, & has occasioned <u>his</u> being disinherited."

* Mrs. Day
* Mrs. Duer
* the Mrs. Pollens
* Mrs. Heywood
* Booths

"Our party at Mrs Duer's produced the novelties of two old Mrs Pollens & Mrs Heywood, with whom my Mother made a Quadrille Table; & of Mrs Maitland & Caroline, & Mr Booth without his sisters at Commerce.—I have got a Husband for each of the Miss Maitlands;—Coln Powlett & his Brother have taken Argyle's inner House, & the consequence is so natural that I have no ingenuity *in planning it. If the Brother shd luckily be a little sillier than the Colonel, what a treasure for Eliza!"*

* The Misses Ballard

"The Miss Ballards are said to be remarkably well-informed; their manners are unaffected & pleasing, but they do not talk quite freely enough to be agreable—nor can I discover any right they had by Taste or Feeling to go their late tour."

* Lyell family

"Mrs Lyell's 130 Guineas rent have made a great impression. To the purchase of furniture, whether here or there, she is quite reconciled, & talks of the <u>Trouble</u> as the only evil."

* Miss Cotterel

"Everybody who comes to Southampton finds it either their duty or pleasure to call upon us; Yesterday we were visited by the eldest Miss Cotterel, just arrived from Waltham."

* Mr. Chambers
* Mr. Wren

"My Mother is preparing mourning for Mrs E.K.—she has picked her old silk pelisse to peices, & means to have it dyed black for a gown—a very interesting scheme, tho' just now a little injured by finding that it must be placed in Mr Wren's hands, for Mr Chambers is gone."

* Mr. Floor

"As for Mr Floor, he is at present rather low in our estimation."

- Miss Weathered
- Wallops
- Dr. Percival

"The Wallops are returned. Mr John Harrison has paid his visit of duty & is gone. We have got a new Physician, a Dr Percival, the son of a famous Dr Percival, of Manchester, who wrote Moral Tales for Edward to give to me."

- The Misses Baker

"One Miss Baker makes my gown & the other my Bonnet, which is to be silk covered with Crape."

- Dr. Mant

"Martha & Dr Mant are as bad as ever; he runs after her in the street to apologise for having spoken to a Gentleman while <u>she</u> was near him the day before.——Poor Mrs Mant can stand it no longer; she is retired to one of her married Daughter's."

- Misses Curling

"In the first place, Miss Curling is actually at Portsmouth——which I was always in hopes would not happen.——I wish her no worse, however, than a long & happy abode there. <u>Here</u> she wd probably be dull, & I am sure she wd be troublesome."

- The Misses Lance

"There were only 4 dances, & it went to my heart that the Miss Lances (one of them too named Emma!) should have partners only for two."

- Captain D'Auvergne and friend

"You will not expect to hear that <u>I</u> was asked to dance——but I was——by the Gentleman whom we met <u>that Sunday</u> with Captn D'auvergne. We have always

kept up a Bowing acquaintance since, & being pleased with his black eyes, I spoke to him at the Ball, which brought on me this civility; but I do not know his name,——& he seems so little at home in the English Language that I believe his black eyes may be the best of him. Captain D'Auvergne has got a ship."

* Mr. and Mrs. Hill

"Mrs Hill called on my Mother yesterday while we were gone to Chiswell——& in the course of the visit asked her whether she knew anything of a Clergyman's family of the name of <u>Alford</u> who had resided in our part of Hampshire."

* Mrs. Drew
* Miss Hook
* Mr. Wynne
* Mr. Fitzhugh

"We spent friday Eveng with our friends at the Boarding House, & our curiosity was gratified by the sight of their fellow-inmates, Mrs Drew & Miss Hook, Mr Wynne & Mr. Fitzhugh; the latter is brother to Mrs Lance, & very much the Gentleman."

* Miss Murden
* Mrs. Hookey

"Miss Hook is a wellbehaved, genteelish woman; Mrs Drew wellbehaved, without being at all genteel. Mr Wynne seems a chatty, & rather familiar young man.——Miss Murden was quite a different creature this last Eveng from what she had been before, oweing to her having with Martha's help found a situation in the morng, which bids very fair for comfort: when she leaves Steventon, she comes to board & lodge with Mrs Hookey, the Chemist——for there is no Mr Hookey."

♦ Captain Smith

"I propose being asked to dance by our acquaintance Mr Smith, now Captain Smith, who has lately re-appeared in Southampton, but I shall decline it."

CHAWTON, HAMPSHIRE

About fifteen miles southeast of Steventon

"There were a few families living in the village—but no great intimacy was kept up with any of them—they were on <u>friendly</u> but rather <u>distant</u> terms with all."

—CAROLINE AUSTEN

♦ Hardings

"Mrs Terry, Mary & Robert, with my Aunt Harding & her Daughter, came from Dummer for a day & a night—all very agreable & very much delighted with the new House, & with Chawton in general."

CHAWTON COTTAGE, FROM THE GARDEN.

- Harriet Benn

"You have sometimes expressed a wish of making Miss Benn some present;— Cassandra & I think that something of the Shawl kind to wear over her Shoulders within doors in very cold weather might be useful, but it must not be very handsome or she would not use it. Her long Fur tippet is almost worn out."

- Middletons
- Miss Papillon

"Miss Papillon called on us yesterday, looking handsomer than ever.—Maria Middleton & Miss Benn dine here tomorrow."

- Mr. Peach

"And it is said that Mr Peach (beautiful Wiseacre) wants to have the Curacy of Overton; & if he <u>does</u> leave Wootton, James Digweed wishes to go there.

- Plumptres

"We cannot agree as to which is the eldest of the two Miss Plumbtres;—send us word."

- Webb family

"I return to my Letter writing from calling on Miss Harriot Webb, who is short & not quite straight, & cannot pronounce an R any better than her Sisters— but she has dark hair, a complexion to suit, & I think, has the pleasantest countenance & manner of the three—the most natural."

- Prowting family

"Mr Prowting has opened a Gravel pit, very conveniently for my Mother, just at the mouth of the approach to his House—but it looks a little as if he meant to catch all his company. Tolerable Gravel."

• Mrs. Budd

"Mrs Budd died on Sunday Eveng. I saw her two days before her death, & thought it must happen soon. She suffered much from weakness & restlessness almost to the last."

• Coleby

"There was no ready-made Cloak at Alton that would do, but Coleby has undertaken to supply one in a few days; it is to be Grey Woollen & cost ten shillings."

• Mr. Twyford
• Mr. Wilkes

"We were Eleven altogether, as you will find on computation, adding Miss Benn & two strange Gentlemen, a Mr Twyford, curate of Gt Worldham, who is living in Alton, & his friend Mr Wilkes.—I do not know that Mr T. is anything except very dark-complexioned, but Mr W. was a useful addition, being an easy, talking, pleasantish young Man—a <u>very</u> young Man, hardly 20 perhaps."

• The Misses Sibley

"The Miss Sibleys want to establish a Book Society in their side of the Country, like ours. What can be a stronger proof of that superiority in ours over the Manydown & Steventon society, which I have always foreseen & felt?—No emulation of the kind was ever inspired by <u>their</u> proceedings; no such wish of the Miss Sibleys was ever heard, in the course of the many years of that Society's existence."

• Garnetts

"Dame G. is pretty well, & we found her surrounded by her well-behaved, healthy, large-eyed Children. I took her an old Shift & promised her a set of our Linen; & my Companion left some of her Bank Stock with her."

* Mr. Cottrell

"Mrs Bramstone is the sort of Woman I detest.——Mr Cottrell is worth ten of her."

* Mrs. Edwards
* Mr. and Miss Woolls

"Before I set out we were visited by Mrs Edwards, & while I was gone Miss Beckford & Maria, & Miss Woolls & Harriet B. called, all of whom my Mother was glad to see & I very glad to escape."

* Miss Clewes
* Mrs. Sayce

"The three Miss Knights & Mrs Sayce are just off;——the weather has got worse since the early morng,——& and whether Miss Clewes & I are to be Tete a Tete, or to have 4 gentlemen to admire us is uncertain."

* Mr. and Mrs. Philmore

"Old Philmore I beleive is well again."

* Sclater family

"Kill poor Mrs Sclater if you like it, while you are at Manydown."

* Farmer Andrews

"Poor Farmer Andrews! I am very sorry for him, & sincerely wish his recovery."

* Mr. Louch
* Dusautoys

"We have called upon Miss Dusautoy & Miss Papillon & been very pretty.——Miss D. has a great idea of being Fanny Price, she & her youngest sister together, who is named Fanny."

+ Palmers

"Mr Palmer spent yesterday with us, and is gone off with Cassy this morng."

+ Mr. Sweny
+ Dr. White
+ Sir Thomas Miller
+ Mrs. Baverstock
+ Papillon family

"I am happy to tell you that Mr Papillon will soon make his offer, probably next Monday, as he returns on Saturday.—His <u>intention</u> can be no longer doubtful in the smallest degree, as he has secured the refusal of the House which Mrs Baverstock at present occupies in Chawton & is to vacate soon, which is of course intended for Mrs Elizth Papillon."

+ Sally Benham
+ Caroline Wiggetts
+ Mrs. Calker
+ Triggs

"Old Philmore was buried yesterday, & I, by way of saying something to Triggs, observed that it had been a very handsome Funeral, but his manner of reply made me suppose that it was not generally esteemed so. I can only be sure of <u>one</u> part being very handsome, Triggs himself, walking behind in his Green Coat.— Mrs Philmore attended as chief Mourner, in Bombasin, made very short, and flounced with Crape."

WINCHESTER, HAMPSHIRE

* Mr. Giles King Lyford

"The consequence is, that instead of going to Town to put myself into the hands of some Physician as I shd otherwise have done, I am going to Winchester instead, for some weeks to see what Mr Lyford can do farther towards re-establishing me in tolerable health."

* Dr. Gabell
* Heathcotes

"We see Mrs Heathcote every day, & William is to call upon us soon.——God bless you, my dear Edward."

TIMELINE OF WHERE SHE LIVED AND TRAVELED

STEVENTON RECTORY 1775-1801

DESTINATION	COMPANIONS	DATES
Mrs. Cawley's boarding school, Oxford, then Southampton	Cassandra and cousin Jane Cooper	March–September 1783
Abbey House School, Reading, Berkshire	Cassandra and cousin Jane Cooper	July 1785–December 1786

DESTINATION	COMPANIONS	DATES
Red House, Sevenoaks, Kent, home of Francis Austen, her great uncle, and then London	Her parents and Cassandra	July–early August 1788
Southampton, home of the Butler-Harrison family	Cassandra	December 1793
Adlestrop, Gloucestershire, home of her aunt and uncle Reverend Thomas and Mary Leigh		July 1794
Kent	Cassandra	Summer 1794
Harpsden, Oxfordshire, home of her cousin Edward Cooper		April 20, 1796
Cork Street, London	Brothers Edward and Frank	August 1796
Rowling, Kent, at her brother Edward's		August 25–late September, 1796
1 Paragon Buildings, Bath, at her aunt and uncle's, the Leigh-Perrots	Her mother and sister	November–December 1797
Godmersham, Kent, at her brother Edward's	Her parents and sister	August–October 1798
13 Queen Square, Bath	Her mother, brother Edward, and his wife, Elizabeth	May–June 1799

DESTINATION	COMPANIONS	DATES
Ibthorpe, home of the Lloyds, on the way to Bath	Her family	May 1801

4 SYDNEY PLACE, BATH, SUMMER 1801-MIDSUMMER 1804

DESTINATION	COMPANIONS	DATES
1 Paragon Buildings, at the Leigh-Perrots, before they rented Sydney Place	Her parents and sister	May 1801
Devonshire	Her family	Summer 1801
Steventon, now the home of her brother James		September 1801
Dawlish, Devonshire	Her parents, Cassandra, and brother Charles	Summer 1802
Steventon	Cassandra	September 1–early October 1802
Godmersham	Cassandra and Charles	September 3–October 28, 1802
Steventon		October 28, 1802
Manydown, home of the Bigg sisters and their brother Harris Bigg-Wither	Cassandra	November 25–December 3, 1802

Destination	Companions	Dates
Godmersham	Cassandra	Mid-September–mid-October 1803
Ashe Rectory, home of the Lefroys		October 1803
Lyme Regis, Dorsetshire	Her family	November 1803
Lyme Regis	Her family	August–September 1804

3 GREEN PARK BUILDINGS EAST, BATH, OCTOBER 25, 1804-MARCH 25, 1805

25 GAY STREET, BATH, MARCH 25, 1805-MARCH 13, 1806

Destination	Companions	Dates
Godmersham via Steventon	Her mother and sister	June–September 1805
Worthing, West Sussex	Her family	September–November 1805
Steventon		January 1806

TRIM STREET, BATH, JANUARY 29-JULY 2, 1806

DESTINATION	COMPANIONS	DATES
Manydown	Cassandra	February 1806

NO PERMANENT HOME

DESTINATION	COMPANIONS	DATES
Clifton, Bristol	Cassandra	July–October 1806
Adelstrop, Gloucestershire, home of Leigh family		Late July–August 1806
Stoneleigh Abbey, Warwickshire, home of Leigh family		August 1806
Hamstall Ridware, Staffordshire, home of the Edward Cooper family		August–October 1806
Steventon		October 1806

STONELEIGH ABBEY

TEMPORARY LODGINGS, SOUTHAMPTON, OCTOBER 10, 1806-MARCH 10, 1807

CASTLE SQUARE, SOUTHAMPTON, MARCH 1807-JULY 7, 1809

DESTINATION	COMPANIONS	DATES
Chawton Estate, Edward's property	Her mother and sister	September 1–11, 1807
Manydown	Cassandra	Late December 1807 or early 1808
Steventon	Cassandra	February 1808
Kintbury, home of the Fowles	Cassandra	February 25, 1808
Steventon	Brother Henry	May 16, 1808
16 Michael's Place, Brompton, London	Henry	May–June 1808
Godmersham		June 15–July 8, 1808
Canterbury		June 23 and 24, 1808
Godmersham		May 15–June 30, 1809

CHAWTON COTTAGE,
JULY 7, 1809-MAY 24, 1817

DESTINATION	COMPANIONS	DATES
64 Sloane Street, London, at brother Henry's house		Late March–early May 1811
Streatham, Surrey		Early May, 1811
Steventon	Brother Edward	November 26–30, 1811
Steventon	Her mother	June 9–25, 1812
64 Sloane Street, London, Henry's home		April 22–May 1, 1813
64 Sloane Street, London		May 19–26, 1813
Steventon	Henry	May 28–June 1, 1813
10 Henrietta Street, London, Henry's home		September 14–17, 1813
Godmersham		September 17–November 1813
Canterbury		October 22, 1813
Canterbury		November 2, 1813
London		November 15, 1813
Farnham, Guildford, and Cobham, on the way to London		March 1, 1814
10 Henrietta Street, London		March 2–early April 1814

DESTINATION	COMPANIONS	DATES
Streatham, Surrey, home of Catherine Bigg Hill		Early April 1814
Great Bookham, Surrey, at the Cookes'	Her second cousins	June 24, 1814
23 Hans Place, London, Henry's home		August 22–September 3, 1814
23 Hans Place, London		November 25–December 5, 1814
Winchester, home of Mrs. Heathcote	Cassandra	December 26, 1814
Steventon and Ashe Rectory	Cassandra	January 2–16, 1815
23 Hans Place, London		August 21–September 3, 1815
Steventon	Henry	September 3–8, 1815
23 Hans Place, London		October 4–December 16, 1815
Cheltenham Spa, Gloucestershire	Cassandra	May 23–early June 1816
Kintbury, the Fowle home	Cassandra	Early June 1816
Steventon		June 11–15, 1816
College Street, Winchester		May 24–July 17, 1817

WHO SHE MET ON HER TRAVELS

* Home of the Bridges family, Rowling, Kent, September 1796
  * Brook Bridges
  * Edward Bridges
  * George Bridges
  * Harriot Bridges
  * Henry Bridges
  * Louisa Bridges
  * Marianne Bridges
  * Mr. and Mrs. Bridges
  * Fanny Cage
  * Mr. and Mrs. Cage
  * George Children
  * John Children
  * Mr. Children
  * Mr. Clayton
  * Aunt Fielding
  * Mary Finch
  * Miss Fletcher
  * Caroline Hales
  * Harriet Hales
  * Lady Hales
  * Richard Harvey
  * Miss Holwell
  * Mrs. Joan Knatchbull
  * Lucy Lefroy
  * Archdeacon Lynch
  * Mr. and Mrs. Milles
  * Mary Pearson
  * Richis
  * Mr. Scott
  * Seward
  * Toke family
  * Lady Waltham

* Queen Square, Bath, May–June 1799
  * Mrs. Bromley
  * Mrs. Dowdeswell
  * Mr. and Mrs. Evelyn
  * Dr. and Mrs. Fellowes
  * Mrs. Foley
  * Mr. Gould
  * Dr. Hall
  * Dr. Mapleton
  * The Misses Mapleton
  * Miss North
  * Mrs. Williams
  * Lady Willoughby

* Lyme Regis, September 1804
  * Miss Armstrong
  * Barnewalls

- Miss Bonham
- Mr. Carpenter
- Le Chevalier
- Coles
- Miss Anna Cove and her mother
- Mr. Crawford

- Mrs. Feaver
- Mr. and Mrs. Granville
- Miss Irvine
- Mr. and Mrs. Mawhood
- Mr. Pyne
- Schuylers

Godmersham, Kent, August 1805

- Mr. Brett
- Mrs. Anne Finch
- Lord and Lady Gordon
- Mr. Hall
- Mr. E. Hatton
- Miss Hatton

- Sir Janison
- Knatchbulls
- Mrs. Sace
- Mrs. Salkeld
- Miss Sharp
- Dr. Wilmot

Goodnestone, another home of the Bridges family, August 1805

- Sophie Cage
- Lady Forbes
- Mr. Hammond
- Louisa Hatton

- Charles Knatchbull
- Mr. Sankey
- Captain Woodford

Godmersham, June 1808

- Mrs. and Miss Brydges
- Mr. and Mrs. Filmer
- Annamaria Finch-Hatton
- Charles Graham
- Mr. and Miss Gregory
- Mrs. Hope
- Hughes family

- Mrs. Inman
- Mr. Jefferson
- Widow Kennet
- Dr. Marlowe
- Mrs. C. Milles
- Mr. and Mrs. Moore
- Morrice family
- Lady Catherine Portmore

- Lord Portmore
- Mr. and Mrs. Scudamore
- Jenny Smallbone
- Mr. Waller
- Dr. and Mrs. Walsby
- Mrs. White
- Mr. and Mrs. Whitfield

64 Sloane Street, London, brother Henry's house, April 1811

- Miss Allen
- Sam Arnold
- Miss Beaty
- Miss Beckford
- Lord and Lady Catherine Brecknell
- George and Mary Cooke
- Cookes
- Mr. Cure
- Comte and Madame d'Antraigues
- Miss East
- Henry Egerton
- Mr. Guillemarde
- Mr. Hampson
- Wyndham Knatchbull
- Mrs. Latouche
- Miss Middleton
- Miss Payne
- Miss Emma Plumptre
- The Misses Rolle
- Mr. Seymour
- Captain Simpson
- Colonel and Mrs. Cantelo Smith
- Tilsons
- Henry Walter

64 Sloane Street, London, Henry Austen's, May 1813

- Mr. Barlow
- Charlotte Craven
- Mr. Hampson
- Mr. Herington
- Hoblyn family
- Mrs. Perigord
- Mr. Phillips
- Lady Drummond Smith

10 Henrietta Street, London, Henry's home, September 1813

- Madame Bigeon
- Miss Hare
- Lady Ogleby
- Lady Robert Kerr
- Mr. Spence
- Mr. Spencer
- Mrs. Tickars
- Mr. Edmund Williams

✦ Godmersham, September–November 1813

- Will Amos
- Miss Dora Best
- Mrs. Birch
- Mrs. Breton
- Mr. Brett
- Jemima Brydges
- Mrs. Carrick
- Laura Chapman
- Mrs. Chapman
- Mr. Chisholme
- Mary Croucher
- Mary Doe
- Mrs. Driver
- Fagg family
- Two Mrs. Finches
- Mrs. Fletcher
- Mary Jane Fowle
- Mr. Gipps
- Mrs. Gore
- Mrs. Hamilton
- Hammonds
- Mr. Hawker
- Miss Hawley
- Lady Honeywood
- Edward Hussey
- Mr. Johncock
- Kendall
- Miss Lee
- Dame Libscombe
- Mr. Lushington
- Mr. Robert Mascall
- O'Neil
- Mr. Ogle
- Mr. and Mrs. Osborne
- Mary Oxenden
- Mr. Paget
- Dr. Parry
- John Plumptre
- Mr. and Mrs. Sherer
- Mary Stacey
- Tyldens
- Miss Wemyss
- Mr. Wigram
- Miss Wildman
- Mrs. Wildman

✦ Henrietta Street, London, March 1814

- General Chownes
- Miss Spencer
- Mr. and Mrs. John Warren
- Mr. Wickham
- J. Wildman

    ✦   23 Hans Place, London, Henry's home, August–September 1814

"I live in his room downstairs, it is particularly pleasant, from opening upon the garden. I go and refresh myself every now & then, and then come back to Solitary Coolness."

- Birches
- Miss Burdett
- Crutchleys
- Lady Charlotte Graham

    ✦   23 Hans Place, London, November 1814

- Mr. Hayter
- Mr. Sanford

    ✦   23 Hans Place, London, October–December 1815

- James Stanier Clarke
- Creeds
- Maria Cuthbert
- Mr. Gordon
- Charles Thomas Haden
- Herries
- Mrs. Hore
- Mr. Jackson
- Malings
- Mr. Meyer

STATELY MANSIONS IN HER LIFE

- Goodnestone, Kent, home of Edward Knight's in-laws, the Bridges
- Adlestrop, Gloucestershire, home Mrs. Austen's cousin, Reverend Thomas Leigh
- Stoneleigh Abbey, Warwickshire, home of other Leigh cousins of Mrs. Austen
- Godmersham, Kent, Edward Knight's estate
- Chawton House, Hampshire, another home of Edward Knight

CULTURAL OUTINGS IN LONDON

- Astley's Amphitheatre, equestrian circus
- Covent Garden
  - *Artaxerxes*, an opera by Thomas Arne
  - *Clandestine Marriage*, by George Coleman
  - *The Devil to Pay*, by Charles Coffey
  - *The Farmer's Wife*, by Charles Dibdin
  - *Isabella*, by David Garrick
  - *Hamlet*, by William Shakespeare
  - *MacBeth*, by William Shakespeare
  - *Midas: an English Burletta*, by Kane O'Hara
  - *Richard III*, by William Shakespeare
- Lyceum Theatre
  - *The Beehive*, by J. V. Millingen
  - *The Boarding House, or Five Hours at Brighton*, by Samuel Beazley
  - *Don Juan, or the Libertine Destroyed*, by Thomas Shadwell
  - *The Hippocrate*, by Isaac Bickerstaffe
- Drury Lane Theatre
  - *Illusion, or the Trances of Nourjahad*, by Robert William Elliston
  - *Merchant of Venice*, by William Shakespeare
- Liverpool Museum
- Great Exhibition, Somerset House
- Exhibition at Spring Gardens, watercolors
- British Gallery, Pall Mall
  - *Christ Healing the Sick*, by Benjamin West
- Pall Mall exhibition, Joshua Reynolds paintings

- 125 Pall Mall
  - *Christ Rejected*, by Benjamin West
- Home of Comte d'Antraigues, opera singer wife, and son Julien
- Carlton House, Prince Regent's town residence
  - Tour by librarian of Carlton House, James Stanier Clarke

POSSESSIONS

BOOKS SHE OWNED

From *A Bibliography of Jane Austen* by David Gilson

- *The Spectator*, Vol. 6, 1744
- *Orlando furioso: Translated from the Italian; with Notes*, John Hoole, Lodovico Ariosto, 1783
- *Hermsprong; or, Man as He Is Not*, Robert Bage, 1796
- *Travels from Saint Petersburg in Russia, to Diverse Parts of Asia*, John Bell, 1764
- *L'ami des enfans*, Arnaud Berquin, 1782–83
- *L'ami de l'adolescence (suite de L'ami des enfans)*, Arnaud Berquin, 1784–85
- *Camilla; or, A Picture of Youth*, Fanny Burney, 1796
- *Curiosities of Literature*, Isaac D'Israeli, 1791
- *Fables choisies*, Anon., before 1783

Little Goody Two Shoes

- *An History of the Earth, and Animated Nature*, Oliver Goldsmith, 1774
- *The History of England, from Earliest Times to the Death of George II*, Oliver Goldsmith, 1771
- *Poems and Plays*, William Hayley, 1785
- *The History of Goody Two-Shoes*, Anon., ca. 1780
- *The History of England*, David Hume, 1759–62
- *The Prince of Abissinia. A Tale*, Samuel Johnson, 1759
- *The Works of the Marchioness de Lambert. Carefully Translated from the French*, Anne Thérèse Lambert, 1749
- *The History of Sir Charles Grandison*, Samuel Richardson, 1754
- *The Works of James Thomson, with His Last Corrections and Improvements*, James Thomson, 1773
- *A Companion to the Altar: Shewing the Nature & Necessity of a Sacramental Preparation in Order to Our Worthy Receiving the Holy Communion, to Which Are Added Prayers and Meditations*, William Vickers, 1793?
- *Excursions from Bath*, Richard Warner, 1801

REMAINING ARTIFACTS
Items belonging to her on display at
Jane Austen's House Museum, Chawton Cottage

- Eight music books, some copied out in Jane's hand, some printed music
- Framed lock of her father's hair
- Topaz cross, given to her by brother Charles

- Pinchbeck bracelet of small blue and ivory beads; pinchbeck is an alloy of copper and zinc invented by Christopher Pinchbeck in the 1700s; also known as false gold
- Pink glass muff chain
- Ivory cup and ball
- Mourning brooch with Jane's hair, inscribed "JA December 16th 1775–July 1817"
- Lock of Jane's hair
- Tripod writing table

"After we had been here a quarter of an hour it was discovered that my writing and dressing boxes had been by accident put into a chaise which was just packing off as we came in, and were driven away towards Gravesend in their way to the West Indies. No part of my property could have been such a prize before, for in my writing-box was all my worldly wealth, 7l., and my dear Harry's deputation."

—JANE TO CASSANDRA, OCTOBER 24, 1798,
FROM THE BULL AND GEORGE IN DARTFORD

- Her Writing Desk
  · Portable writing desk owned by Jane Austen
  · Currently housed at the British Library

❖ Jane's Pelisse

- Pelisse, a coat worn over a dress or gown, owned by Jane Austen c. 1814
- Currently housed at the Hampshire Museum
- Silk
- Twill weave
- Small repeat pattern of oak leaves in gold on warm brown background
- Oak-leaf motif was popular at the time and symbolized the strength of the navy and the nation as a whole
- Long sleeves gathered at the top but close fitting at the elbow
- Bright yellow cord along the front edge and around the wrists
- High standing collar
- Open front with no fastenings
- Lined in white silk

"In around 1875 Jane's niece Marianne Knight was visited by a family friend, Miss Eleanor Glubbe, later Mrs Steele. Marianne gave the pelisse to Miss Glubbe during the visit. In later years Mrs Steele wished to return the pelisse to the Austen family and sent it to Mrs Winifred Jenkyns, a great granddaughter of James Austen, Jane's eldest brother, with a note that reads, 'I missed the little coat for a long time but lately it turned up. I cannot remember if it was "Jane's" but it seems probable.'

"This particular pelisse was presumably given to Edward by Cassandra then handed down to his daughter, Marianne. That she gave it to her friend, Miss Glubbe, who made sure that it was returned to the Austen / Knight family argues an acknowledged obligation on her part. The pelisse was then handed down through the family until 1993, when it was given to the Hampshire County Council Arts & Museums Service."

—HAMPSHIRE MUSEUMS SERVICE

JANE AUSTEN'S RING

TURQUOISE RING PURCHASED AT AUCTION BY AMERICAN POP SINGER KELLY CLARKSON ON JULY 10, 2012 BOUGHT FOR £152,450, ABOUT $236,000

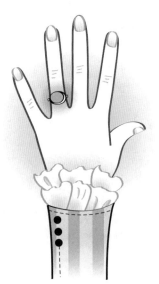

SOTHEBY'S CATALOGUE
NOTES & PROVENANCE

PRINT LOT 59, AUSTEN, JANE. A GOLD AND GEM SET RING

152,450 GBP (Hammer Price with Buyer's Premium)

Set with a cabochon blue stone, natural turquoise, size K½ with sizing band, once belonging to Jane Austen, in a contemporary jeweller's box ("T. West | Goldsmith | Ludgate Street | near St Paul's")

With an autographed note signed by Eleanor Austen, to her niece Caroline Austen, 'My dear Caroline. The enclosed Ring once belonged to your Aunt Jane. It was given to me by your Aunt Cassandra as soon as she knew that I was engaged to your Uncle. I bequeath it to you. God bless you!', November 1863, with address panel on verso and remains of black wax seal impression, fold tears; also with three further notes by Mary Dorothy Austen-Leigh detailing the ring's later provenance, 5 pages, 1935–1962.

PROVENANCE: Jane Austen (1775–1817); her sister Cassandra (1773–1845); given in 1820 to her sister-in-law Eleanor Austen (née Jackson), second wife of Rev. Henry Thomas Austen (d. 1864); given in 1863 to her niece Caroline Mary Craven Austen (1805–1880, the daughter of Rev. James Austen); her niece Mary A. Austen-Leigh (perhaps first to her mother Emma Austen-Leigh, née Smith); her niece Mary Dorothy Austen-Leigh; given to her sister Winifred Jenkyns on 27 March 1962; thence by descent.

CATALOGUE NOTE: An intimate personal possession of Jane Austen's, hitherto unknown to scholars, that has remained with the author's descendants until the present day. The stone has been identified as natural turquoise but was initially thought to be odontalite, a form of fossilised dentine that has been heated to give it a distinctive blue colour, which came into fashion in the early 19th century as a substitute for turquoise. It is an attractive but simply designed piece, befitting not only its owner's modest income but also what is known of her taste in jewellery.

On Jane's death her jewellery, along with other personal possessions, passed to Cassandra, and she appears to have given a number of pieces as mementos."

THINGS SHE MADE

- Framed lock of her father's hair
- Needle case inscribed "With Aunt Jane's love"
- Embroidered lace collar
- Handkerchief embroidered with floral sprig and initials C.A.
- Indian muslin scarf embroidery
- Patchwork quilt made by Jane, Cassandra, and Mrs. Austen

"Have you remembered to collect pieces for the Patchwork?"

—JANE TO CASSANDRA, MAY 31, 1811

KNOWN REMAINING MANUSCRIPTS AND LETTERS

- *Juvenilia*, 1787–1793
  - *Volume the First* housed at the Bodleian Library, Oxford
  - *Volume the Second*, British Library
  - *Volume the Third*, British Library
- *The History of England*, 1791, British Library
- *Sir Charles Grandison or The Happy Man, a Comedy*, Chawton House Library
- *Lady Susan*, complete draft, paper watermark of 1805, Morgan Library
- *Susan* title page, *Susan* is the precursor to *Northanger Abbey*, 1803?, Morgan Library
- *The Watsons*, about 1804, Morgan Library, Bodleian Library
- *Plan of a Novel*, about 1815, Morgan Library
- *Poem on Captain Foote's marriage to Miss Patten*, in Jane's hand, but composed by her uncle, Morgan Library
- Two chapters of *Persuasion*, 1816, British Library

- *Sanditon*, 1817, Cambridge University
- *Opinions of Mansfield Park*, British Library
- *Opinions of Emma*, British Library
- *Profits of My Novels*, a tally of her earnings, 1817, Morgan Library
- 161 letters

Books She Read

- *Matilda*, a play, Dr. Thomas Francklin
- *Fables*, John Gay
- *Poems on Several Occasions*, Dr. Moss
- *Mentoria; or, The Young Ladies' Instructor*, Ann Murray
- *Moral Tales*, Dr. Thomas Percival
- *Elegant Extracts*, a literary anthology
- *The Rivals*, Richard Brinsley Sheridan
- *The History of Tom Jones, a Foundling*, Henry Fielding, 1749
- *The Mirror*, a journal
- *The Complete Italian Master*, Giovanni Veneroni
- *Mary Queen of Scots Vindicated*, John Whitaker, 1787
- *The Wonder: A Woman Keeps a Secret*, a play, Susannah Centlivre, 1714
- *The Chances*, a play, John Fletcher
- *The Tragedy of Tragedies; or, The Life and Death of Tom Thumb the Great*, play, Henry Fielding, 1731
- *The Sultan*, a play, Isaac Bickerstaffe, 1784
- *High Life Below Stairs*, a play, James Townley, 1759
- *Arthur Fitz-Albini*, Egerton Brydges, 1798

"We have got 'Fitz-Albini'; my father has bought it against my private wishes, for it does not quite satisfy my feelings that we should purchase the only one of Egerton's works of which his family are ashamed. That these scruples, however, do not at all interfere with my reading it, you will easily believe. We have neither of us yet finished the first volume. My father is disappointed—I am not, for I expected nothing better."

—JANE TO CASSANDRA, NOVEMBER 25, 1798

- *The Lady's Monthly Museum* (1798–99), essay "Effects of Mistaken Synonymy" included headline "Sense and Sensibility"
- *Belinda*, Maria Edgeworth (1801)
- Poetry of George Crabbe
- *Marmion* (1808), Sir Walter Scott
- *Evelina; or, the History of a Young Lady's Entrance into the World* (1778), Frances Burney
- *Lady Maclairn, the Victim of Villainy* (1806), Hunter of Norwich
- *Travels in Spain* (1809), Sir John Carr
- *The Heroine; or, Adventures of a Fair Romance Reader* (1813), E. S. Barrett
- *An Account of the Manner and Customs of Italy and A Journey from London to Genoa* (1768), Joseph Baretti
- *Life of Lord Macartney, with Extracts from an Account of the Russian Empire, the Political History of Ireland and the Journal of an Embassy to China* (1807), Sir John Barrow
- *The Hermit* (1766) and *The Minstrel* (1771–74), James Beattie
- *Letters on the Modern History and Political Aspects of Europe* (1804), *History of Spain* (1810), and *A System of Geography and History* (1812), John Bigland

+ *Journal of a Tour to the Hebrides* (1785) and *Life of Samuel Johnson* (1791, 1793), James Boswell
+ *Self-control* (1810), Mary Brunton
+ *Christian Researches in Asia* (1811), Claudius Buchanan
+ *Cecelia; or, Memoirs of an Heiress* (1782), Fanny Burney
+ *Clarentine* (1798), Sarah Harriet Burney
+ *Life of James II* (1816) and *Sermons Preached in the Western Squadron* (1798), James Stanier Clarke
+ *The Shipwreck* (1804), William Falconer
+ *History of the Abolition of the African Slave Trade* (1808), Thomas Clarkson
+ *The Tour of Dr. Syntax in Search of the Picturesque: A Poem* (1812), William Combe
+ *Battleridge, an Historical Tale Founded on Facts, by a Lady of Quality* (1799), Cassandra Cooke
+ *Examination of the Necessity of Sunday-drilling* (1803), *Sermons, Chiefly Designed to Elucidate* (1804), *Practical and Familiar Sermons* (1809), and *Two Sermons Preached at Wolverhampton* (1816), Reverend Edward Cooper
+ *The Borough* (1810) and *Tales* (1812), George Crabbe
+ *Alphonsine; ou, La tendresse maternelle* (1806) and *Les Veillées du Chateau* (1784), Madame de Genlis
+ *Lettres de Mme de Sévigné* (1726), Madame de Sévigné
+ *Corinne; ou, L'Italie* (1807), Madame de Stael
+ *Robinson Crusoe* (1719), Daniel Defoe
+ *Collection of Poems in Six Volumes by Several Hands* (1758), Robert Dodsley
+ *The Peacock's "At Home"* (1807), Catherine Ann Dorset
+ *Patronage* (1814), Maria Edgeworth

- *Enquiry into the Duties of the Female Sex* (1797), Thomas Gisborne
- *Caleb Williams* (1794) and *St. Leon* (1799), William Godwin
- *The Vicar of Wakefield* (1766), Oliver Goldsmith
- *Letters from the Mountains; Being the Real Correspondence of a Lady between the Years 1773 and 1803* (1807) and *Memoirs of an American Lady* (1808), Anne Grant
- Writings of Elizabeth Hamilton
- *Cantabrigia Depicta* (1809–11), R. B. Harraden
- *Rosanne; or, A Father's Labour Lost* (1814), Laetitia Hawkins
- *The History of Great Britain, from the First Invasion of It by the Romans under Julius Caesar* (1771–93), Robert Henry
- *Guida di Musica, Being a Complete Book of Instruction for the Harpsichord or Pianoforte* (1790), James Hook
- *Letters from Mrs. Palmerstone to Her Daughter Inculcating Morality by Entertaining Narratives* (1803), Rachel Hunter
- *Two Sermons* (1808), Reverend Thomas Jefferson
- Pamphlet on cowpox (1798–1800), Dr. Edward Jenner
- *Tableau de famille*, Jean de La Fontaine
- *Midnight Bell, a German Story Founded on Incidents in Real Life* (1798), Francis Lathom
- *The Female Quixote; or, The Adventures of Arabella* (1752), Charlotte Lennox
- *Gil Blas* (1715–35), Alain-René Lesage
- *Travels in Iceland* (1811), Lord Macartney and Sir George Mackenzie
- *Paradise Lost* (1667), John Milton
- *Cœlebs in Search of a Wife* (1809) and *Practical Piety* (1811), Hannah More

+ *The Wild Irish Girl* (1806) and *Woman; or, Ida of Athens* (1809), Sydney Owenson (Lady Morgan)
+ *Essay on the Military Policy and Institutions of the British Empire* (1810), Sir Charles William Pasley
+ *Letters to and from the Late Samuel Johnson* (1788), Hester Piozzi
+ *Essay on Man* (1733), Alexander Pope
+ *Lake of Killarney* (1804), Anna Maria Porter
+ *The Mysteries of Udolpho* (1794) and others, Ann Radcliffe
+ *Lady of the Lake* (1810), *Waverley* (1814), *The Field of Waterloo* (1815), *Paul's Letters to His Kinsfolk* (1815), and *The Antiquary* (1816), Sir Walter Scott
+ *Letters from Italy* (1766), Samuel Sharp
+ *Several Discourses Preached at the Temple Church* (1812), Thomas Sherlock
+ *Rejected Addresses; or, The New Theatrum Poetarum* (1812), James and Horatio Smith
+ *Letters from England, by Don Manuel Alvarez Espriella* (1807)
+ *The Life of Nelson* (1896), and *The Poet's Pilgrimage to Waterloo* (1816), Robert Southey
+ *Tristram Shandy* (1760–67), Laurence Sterne
+ *Gulliver's Travels* (1726), Jonathan Swift
+ *Margiana, or Widdrington Tower* (1808), Henrietta Sykes
+ *Four Letters on Important National Subjects* (1783), Reverend Dr. Josiah Tucker
+ *Alicia de Lacy: An Historical Romance* (1814), Jane West
+ *Narrative of the Events Which Have Taken Place in France* (1815), Helen Maria Williams

FLOWERS IN HER GARDENS

"Our young Piony at the foot of the Fir tree has just blown & looks very handsome; & the whole of the Shrubbery Border will soon be gay with Pinks & Sweet Williams, in addition to the Columbines already in bloom."

—JANE TO CASSANDRA, MAY 29, 1811, FROM CHAWTON COTTAGE

* Lilacs
* Peonies
* Sweet Williams
* Pinks
* Columbines

* Syringas or Philadelphus (mock orange)
* Laburnum
* Mignonette

"Some of the Flower seeds are coming up very well—but your Mignionette makes a wretched appearance."

—JANE TO CASSANDRA, MAY 29, 1811, FROM CHAWTON

* Cornflowers
* Hollyhocks
* Roses

* Sweetbriar
* Small daisies

FRUITS AND VEGETABLES IN HER GARDENS

"Yesterday I had the agreable surprise of finding several scarlet strawberries quite ripe;—had you been at home, this would have been a pleasure lost. There

are more Gooseberries & fewer Currants than I thought at first.—We must buy currants for our Wine."

—Jane to Cassandra, June 6, 1811

- Peas
- Tomatoes
- Potatoes

- Gooseberries
- Currants

"I gather some Currants every now & then, when I want either fruit or employment."

- Strawberries
- Orleans plums
- Greengages

- Apricots
- Mulberries

"I will not say that your Mulberry trees are dead, but I am afraid they are not alive. We shall have pease soon."

- Raspberries

Animals Belonging to the Austens

- Squirrel, a pony bought by brother Frank when he was seven
- Pigs
- Sheep

- Turkeys
- Ducks
- Chickens
- Guinea fowls

"Edw:d desires his Love to You, to Grandpapa, to Anna, to little Edw:d, to Aunt James & Uncle James, & he hopes all your Turkies & Ducks & Chicken & Guinea Fowls are very well."

- Chaffinch
- Bees

"In what part of Bath do you mean to place your <u>Bees</u>?"

—JANE TO CASSANDRA

- Brown mare
- Mr. Skipsey, horse
- Black mare
- Cows
- Hugh Capet, horse
- Donkeys

"Sixty one Guineas & a half for the three Cows gives one some support under the blow of only Eleven Guineas for the Tables."

WHAT SHE ATE AND DRANK

"My mother desires me to tell you that I am a very good housekeeper, which I have no reluctance in doing, because I really think it my peculiar excellence, and for this reason—I always take care to provide such things as please my own appetite, which I consider as the chief merit in housekeeping. I have had some ragout veal, and I mean to have some haricot mutton to-morrow. We are to kill a pig soon."

- Turkey
- Cold souse

"Caroline, Anna & I have just been devouring some cold Souse, & it would be difficult to say which enjoyed it most."

- Liqueurs
- Venison
- Beefsteaks
- Boiled fowl
- Boiled chicken
- Ragout veal
- Haricot mutton
- Oxcheek
- Dumplings
- Pease soup
- Spareribs
- Pudding
- Tea
- Asparagus & a lobster
- Cheesecakes

"At Devizes we had comfortable rooms, & a good dinner to which we sat down about 5; amongst other things we had Asparagus & a Lobster which made me wish for you, & some cheesecakes on which the children made so delightful a supper as to endear the Town of Devizes to them for a long time."

- Gooseberry pie
- Gooseberry pudding
- Wine
- Sandwiches allover mustard

"I beleive I drank too much wine last night at Hurstbourne; I know not how else to account for the shaking of my hand to day."

+ Bath buns   + Mead

"We must husband our present stock of Mead; & I am sorry to perceive that our 20 Gal: is very nearly out.——I cannot comprehend how the 14 Gal: cd last so long."

+ Toasted cheese   + Rice pudding
+ Apple dumplings

"When you receive this, our guests will be all gone or going; and I shall be left to the comfortable disposal of my time, to ease of mind from the torments of rice puddings and apple dumplings, and probably to regret that I did not take more pains to please them all."

+ Boiled leg of mutton   + Bad butter

"At Dartford, which we reached within the two hours and three-quarters, we went to the Bull, the same inn at which we breakfasted in that said journey, and on the present occasion had about the same bad butter."

+ Tart and jelly

"Mr K. went away early;——Mr. Moore succeeded him, & we sat quietly working & talking till 10; when he ordered his wife away, & we adjourned to the Dressing room to eat our Tart & Jelly."

+ Orange wine   + Hare
+ Ice and French wine   + Apple pie
+ Currants   + Widgeon
+ Pheasants   + Preserved ginger
+ Spruce beer   + Black butter

"The Widgeon, & the preserved Ginger were as delicious as one could wish. But as to our Black Butter, do not decoy anybody to Southampton by such a lure, for it is all gone."

- Sole

"Mr Egerton & Mr Walter came at ½ past 5, & the festivities began with a pr of very fine Soals."

- China tea
- Neck of mutton

"I had a few lines from Henry on Tuesday to prepare us for himself & his friend, & by the time that I had made the sumptuous provision of a neck of Mutton on the occasion, they drove into the Court—but lest you should not immediately recollect in how many hours a neck of Mutton may be certainly procured, I add that they came a little after twelve—both tall, & well, & in their different degrees agreable."

- Port and brandy
- Stilton cheese
- Veal cutlets and cold ham
- Coffee
- Soup, fish, *bouillée*, partridges, and an apple tart

"Mde Bigeon was below dressing us a most comfortable dinner of Soup, Fish, Bouillée, Partridges & an apple Tart, which we sat down to soon after 5, after cleaning & dressing ourselves & feeling that we were most commodiously disposed of."

- Soup, wine and water
- Sugar loaf
- Roast fowl
- Venison
- Pickled cucumbers
- Sea kale

"At 7 we set off in a Coach for the Lyceum—were at home again in about 4 hours and 1/2—had Soup & wine & water, & then went to our Holes."

GAMES SHE PLAYED

"We do not want amusement; bilbocatch, at which George is indefatigable, spillikins, paper ships, riddles, conundrums, and cards, with watching the flow and ebb of the river."

—JANE TO CASSANDRA, OCTOBER 24, 1808

+ Spillikins

"She could throw the spilikens for us, better than anyone else, and she was wonderfully successful at cup and ball."

—CAROLINE AUSTEN

+ Paper ships
+ Riddles
+ Rhymes
+ Conundrums
+ Card games
+ Nines

+ Battledore
+ Shuttlecock
+ Bilbocatch
+ Whist
+ Commerce
+ Jeu de violon

"A second pool of Commerce, & all the longer by the addition of the two girls, who during the first had one corner of the Table & Spillikins to themselves, was the ruin of us;—it completed the prosperity of Mr Debary, however, for he won them both."

+ Casino
+ Loo

+ Cribbage
+ Speculation

"Our evening was equally agreeable in its way; I introduced speculation, and it was so much approved that we hardly knew how to leave off."

+ Brag

+ Vingt-un

"*The preference of Brag over Speculation does not greatly surprise me I beleive, because I feel the same myself; but it mortifies me deeply, because Speculation was under my patronage;—& after all, what is there so delightful in a pair royal of Braggers? it is but three nines or three Knaves, or a mixture of them.—When one comes to reason upon it, it cannot stand its ground against Speculation—of which I hope Edward is now convinced.*"

OTHER PASTIMES

- Theatricals with her family and friends at Steventon
  - *Matilda*, a tragedy
  - *The Rivals*, a comedy
  - *Which Is the Man?*
  - *Bon Ton*
  - *The Wonder: A Woman Keeps a Secret*
  - *The Chances*
  - *The Tragedy of Tragedies; or, The Life and Death of Tom Thumb the Great*
  - *The Sultan*
  - *High Life Below Stairs*

- Playing piano

"*Yes, yes, we <u>will</u> have a Pianoforte, as good a one as can be got for 30 Guineas—& I will practise country dances, that we may have some amusement for our nephews & nieces, when we have the pleasure of their company.*"

- Needlework

"*She was fond of work—and she was a great adept at overcast and satin stitch.*"

—CAROLINE AUSTEN

- Concerts

"*The Music was extremely good. It opened (tell Fanny) with 'Prike pe Parp pin praise pof Prapela';—& of the other Glees I remember, 'In peace Love*" tunes,' 'Rosabelle,' 'The red cross Knight,' & 'Poor Insect.' Between the Songs were Lessons on the Harp, or Harp & Piano Forte together—and the Harp Player was Wiepart, whose name seems famous, tho' new to me.—There was one female singer, a short Miss Davis all in blue, bringing up for the Public Line, whose voice was said to be very fine indeed; & all the Performers gave great satisfaction by doing what they were paid for, & giving themselves no airs. No Amateur could be persuaded to do anything."

- Theater
- Art exhibits
- Dances and balls
- Walks
- Fireworks

"We did not go till nine, & then were in very good time for the Fire-works which were really beautiful, & surpassing my expectation;—the illuminations too were very pretty."

- Sewing for charities

HER MUSICAL INSTRUMENT

Pianoforte: she had one, took lessons

"Aunt Jane began her day with music—for which I conclude that she had a natural taste, as she thus kept it up—tho' she had not one to teach; was never induced (as I have heard) to play in company; and none of her family cared much for it. I suppose, that she might not trouble them, she chose her practising time before breakfast—when she could have the room to herself—She practised regularly every morning—She played very pretty tunes, I thought—and I liked to stand by her and listen to them; but the music (for I knew the books well in after years) would now be *thought disgracefully easy—Much that she played was from manuscript, copied out by herself—and so neatly and correctly, that it was as easy to read as print."*

—CAROLINE AUSTEN

SIX OF HER FAVORITE SONGS

(Courtesy of Jeanice Brooks, Professor of Music,
University of Southampton, England)

- "Que j'aime à voir les hirondelles" (text by Jean-Pierre Claris de Florian, music by François Devienne)
- "Their groves o' sweet myrtle" (text by Robert Burns, anonymous musical setting)
- "Oh! No, my love no," from *Of Age To-morrow* (text by Matthew "Monk" Lewis, music by Michael Kelly)
- "The Yellow-haired Laddy" (Scottish song)
- "Queen Mary's Lamentation" (Tommaso Giordani)
- "Robin Adair" (mentioned in *Emma*; keyboard variations by George Kiallmark based on the song are preserved in her keyboard manuscript)

SONGS IN HER MUSIC BOOKS

From *Jane Austen's Music* by Ian Gammie and Derek McCulloch

- Book Two (of eight bound volumes) copied in Jane's hand
- "Ouverture des Pretendus"
- "Fandango É los Gigangas," from *Thicknesse's Tour*
- "Ouverture de Renaud d'Ast"
- "Nos Galen"
- "Mrs. Hamilton of Princaitland's Strathspey"
- "The Austrian Grenadier's Quick March"
- "Troop of the Coldstream Regiment of Guards"

- "The London March"
- "March by Mr. Niger"
- "Scotch Air"
- "The Austrian Retreat"
- "Les Trois Sultanes"
- Two untitled
- Mazzinghi: "Sonata"
- Two waltzes
- "The Duke of York's New March Performed by the Coldstream Regiment"
- "March in Blue Beard"
- Two German waltzes
- "Coolun with Variations"
- "Duke of York's March"
- J. Sterkel: "Sonata by Sterckel"
- Lady Caroline Lee: "The Gloucester Waltz"
- "La Rose" (cotillon)
- "The Perigodine"
- "To Fair Fidele's Grassy Tomb," with variations
- "Old Robin Gray," with variations
- March
- "My Lodging Is on the Cold Ground," duet
- J. Powell: "My Love She's But a Lassie Yet," with variations
- D. Corri: "My Ain Kind Dearie," with variations
- "The Nightingale"
- "Polonese Russe"
- Steibelt: "Steibelt's 10th Pot Pourri," with variations
- Arne: "Overture to Artaxerxes"

HOW SHE SPENT HER DAY
AT CHAWTON

As observed by niece Caroline Austen

"It was a very quiet life according to our ideas but they were readers & besides the housekeeping our Aunts occupied themselves in working for the poor & teaching here & there some boy or girl to read & write."

"Aunt Jane began her day with music."

"She practised regularly every morning."

"I don't believe Aunt Jane observed any particular method in parcelling out her day but I think she generally sat in the drawing room till luncheon; when visitors were there, chiefly at work."

"After luncheon, my Aunts generally walked out—sometimes they went to Alton for shopping—Often, one or the other of them, to the Great House—as it was then called—when a brother was inhabiting it, to make a visit—or if the house were standing empty they liked to stroll about the grounds—sometimes to Chawton Park—a noble beech wood, just within a walk—but sometimes, but that was rarely, to call on a neighbor—They had no carriage, and their visitings did not extend far."

Clothes She Wore

- Headband
- White gloves
- Silk stockings
- Shifts
- Stuff gown (worsted cloth, twill or plain weave, common wool)
- Caps
- Flannel
- Hat
- Mamalouc cap

"I am not to wear my white sattin cap to night after all; I am to wear a Mamalouc cap instead, which Charles Fowle sent to Mary, & which she lends me.—It is all the fashion now, worn at the Opera, & by Lady Mildmays at Hackwood Balls.—I hate describing such things, & I dare say You will be able to guess what it is like.—I have got over the dreadful epocha of Mantuamaking much better than I expected."

- Black cap, narrow silver round it, and coquelicot

"My black cap was openly admired by Mrs. Lefroy, & secretly I imagine by every body else in the room."

- Gown

"My Gown is made very much like my blue one, which you always told me sat very well, with only these variations—the sleeves are short, the wrap fuller, the apron comes over it, & a band of the same completes the whole."

- Shawl
- White satin cap
- Green shoes
- White fan

"I wore my Green shoes last night, & took my <u>white fan</u> with me; I am very glad he never threw it into the River."

- Gown with short sleeves, fuller wrap, apron comes over it
- Petticoat
- Cloak

"My Cloak is come home.…I like it very much, & can now exclaim with delight, like J. Bond at Hay-Harvest, 'This is what I have been looking for these three years.'—I saw some Gauzes in a shop in Bath Street yesterday at only 4s a yard, but they were not so good or so pretty as mine. Flowers are very much worn, & fruit is still more the thing."

- Hat, straw with narrow purple ribbon
- Pink shoes
- Worsted stockings
- Gown, with bit of muslin of the same round her head, bordered with Mrs. Cooper's band and one little comb
- Gown made by Miss Summers
- White gown
- Pink gown

"I shall want two new coloured gowns for the summer, for my pink one will not do more than clear me from Steventon."

- Plain brown cambric muslin

"A plain brown cambric muslin, for morning wear; the other, which is to be a very pretty yellow and white cloud, I mean to buy in Bath. Buy two brown ones, if you please, and both of a length, but one longer than the other—it is for a tall woman. Seven yards for my mother, seven yards and a half for me; a dark brown, but the

kind of brown is left to your own choice, and I had rather they were different, as it will be always something to say, to dispute about which is the prettiest."

* Dark gown
* Crepe sleeves
* Crepe-and-flowers hat or cap

"My Cloak came on tuesday, & tho' I expected a good deal, the beauty of the lace astonished me.——It is too handsome to be worn, almost too handsome to be looked at."

"It is to be a round Gown, with a Jacket, & a Frock front, like Cath: Bigg's, to open at the side.——The Jacket is all in one with the body, & comes as far as the pocketholes;——about half a quarter of a yard deep I suppose all the way round, cut off straight at the Corners with a broad hem.——No fullness appears either in the Body or the flap;——the back is quite plain in this form;——[drawing of a four-sided shape that looks like a vase wider at the top] and the sides equally so.——The front is sloped round to the bosom & drawn in——& and there is to be a frill of the same to put on occasionally when all one's handkercheifs are dirty——which frill <u>must</u> fall back. She is to put two breadths & a half in the tail, & no Gores——Gores not being so much worn as they were;——there is nothing new in the sleeves,——they are to be plain, with a fullness of the same falling down & gathered up underneath, just like some of Marthas——or perhaps a little longer. Low in the back behind, & a belt of the same.——I can think of nothing more——tho' I am afraid of not being particular enough."

HAIRDOS

"I have made myself two or three caps to wear of evenings since I came home, and they save me a world of torment as to hair-dressing, which at present gives me no

trouble beyond washing and brushing, for my long hair is always plaited up out of sight, and my short hair curls well enough to want no papering."

- Wore caps
- Long hair is plaited "up out of sight"
- Short hair "curls well enough to want no papering"
- Cut by Mr. Butler
- Hair cut by Mr. Hall for 2s. 6d.

WHERE SHE WORSHIPPED

- St. Nicholas Church, Steventon
- Godmersham Church

"Do the Ashford people still come to Godmersham Church every Sunday in a cart?"

- Church in Bath
- St. Swithin's, Walcot, Bath
- All Saints Church, Southampton
- Chawton Church

"Oh!—the Church must have looked very forlorn. We all thought of the empty Pew."

- Belgrave Chapel, London
- St. James Church, London
- Winchester Cathedral

WHERE SHE SHOPPED

- Lace man
- John Burdon, bookseller
- Overton Scotchman, fabric and drapery-goods peddler
- London
  - Covent Garden
  - Leicester Square
  - The Strand
- Remnants
- Christian's
- Bedford House (Layton & Shears)
- Mr. Herington's shop, Guildford
- Grafton House
- Crook and Besford's

"I hope you will receive the Gown tomorrow & may be able with tolerable honesty to say that you like the Colour;—it was bought at Grafton House, where, by going very early, we got immediate attendance & went on very comfortably. I only forgot the one particular thing which I had always resolved to buy there—a white silk Handkf—& was therefore obliged to give six shillings for one at Crook & Besford's—which reminds me to say that the Worsteds ought also to be at Chawton tomorrow & that I shall be very happy to hear they are approved."

- Newton's
- Remmington's
- Wedgwood
- Birchall's
- Bracknell & Twinings

Her Health

"Thank you, my Back has given me scarcely any pain for many days.—I have an idea that agitation does it as much harm as fatigue, & that I was ill at the time of your going from the very circumstance of your going.—I am nursing myself up now into as beautiful a state as I can, because I hear that Dr White means to call on me before he leaves the Country."

- Four weeks late at birth
- Putrid fever or epidemic typhus
- Cold and weakness in one of her eyes
- Weak eyes
- Whooping cough
- Ear infection
- Little fever and indisposition
- Back pain
- Bilious attacks

"My dearest Charles

Many thanks for your affectionate Letter. I was in your debt before, but I have really been too unwell the last fortnight to write anything that was not absolutely necessary. I have been suffering from a Bilious attack, attended with a good deal of fever.—A few days ago my complaint appeared removed, but I am ashamed to say that the shock of my Uncle's Will brought on a relapse, & I was so ill on friday & thought myself so likely to be worse that I could not but press for Cassandra's returning with Frank after the funeral last night, which she of course did, & either her return, or my having seen

Mr Curtis, or my Disorder's chusing to go away, have made me better this morning. I live upstairs however for the present & am coddled. I am the only one of the Legatees who has been so silly, but a weak Body must excuse weak Nerves."

Yours Ever truely J.A.

"In my later visits to Chawton Cottage, I remember Aunt Jane used often to lie down after dinner—My Grandmother herself was frequently on the sofa—sometimes in the afternoon, sometimes in the evening, at no fixed period of the day,—She had not bad health for her age, and she worked often for hours in the garden, and naturally wanted rest afterwards—There was only one sofa in the room—and Aunt Jane laid upon 3 chairs which she arranged for herself—I think she had a pillow, but it never looked comfortable—She called it *her* sofa, and even when the <u>other</u> was unoccupied, <u>she</u> never took it—It seemed understood that she preferred the chairs—I wondered and wondered—for the real sofa was frequently vacant, and <u>still</u> she laid in this comfortless manner—I often asked her how she <u>could</u> like the chairs best—and I suppose I worried her into telling me the reason of her choice—which was, that if she ever used the sofa, Grandmama would be leaving it for her, and would not lie down, as she did now, whenever she felt inclined."

—Caroline Austen, March 1867

MORBID SENSE OF HUMOR

"Mrs John Lyford is so much pleased with the state of widowhood as to be going to put in for being a widow again;—she is to marry a Mr Fendall, a banker in

Gloucester, a man of very good fortune, but considerably older than herself & with three little children."

"I have a great mind not to acknowledge the receipt of your letter, which I have just had the pleasure of reading, because I am so ashamed to compare the sprawling lines of this with it!—But if I say all that I have to say, I hope I have no reason to hang myself."

"Mr Waller is dead, I see;—I cannot greive about it, nor perhaps can his Widow very much."

"I had a great mind to add that, if she persisted in giving it, I would spin nothing with it but a Rope to hang myself—but I was afraid of making it appear a less serious matter of feeling than it really is."

"Sir Tho: Miller is dead. I treat you with a dead Baronet almost every Letter."

Pet Peeve: Untidiness

"Mary does not manage matters in such a way as to make me want to lay in myself. She is not tidy enough in her appearance; she has no dressing-gown to sit up in; her curtains are all too thin, and things are not in that comfort and style about her which are necessary to make such a situation an enviable one. Elizabeth was really a pretty object with her nice clean cap put on so tidily and her dress so uniformly white and orderly."

—Jane Austen to Cassandra, November 1798

BALLS AND DANCES SHE ATTENDED

"She was fond of dancing, and excelled in it."

—HENRY AUSTEN

+ Hampshire Club Ball, Basingstoke, Thursday, October 4, 1792
+ Enham House near Andover, home of sister-in-law's aunt, Mrs. Dewar, mid-October 1792
+ Dolphin Inn assembly, Southampton, December 1793
+ Basingstoke assembly, Monday, December 28, 1795
+ Basingstoke assembly, Wednesday, January 6, 1796
+ Harwoods' ball, Manydown, Friday, January 8, 1796
+ Lefroys' ball, Ashe, Friday, January 15, 1796
+ Bridgeses' dance, Goodnestone, Saturday, September 3, 1796

"We were at a Ball on Saturday, I assure you. We dined at Goodnestone & in the Evening danced two Country Dances and the Boulangeries.——I opened the Ball with Edw:d Bridges; the other couples, were Lewis Cage & Harriot, Frank and Louisa, Fanny & George. Eliz:th played one Country dance, Lady Bridges the other, which She made Henry dance with her; and Miss Finch played the Boulangeries."

+ Basingstoke assembly, Thursday, November 22, 1798
+ Basingstoke assembly, Thursday, December 20, 1798

"There were twenty Dances & I danced them all, & without fatigue."

- Lady Dorchester's ball, Kempshott, Tuesday, January 8, 1799
- Basingstoke assembly, Thursday, October 30, 1800
- Lord Portsmouth's ball, Hurstbourne, Wednesday, November 19, 1800
- Upper Rooms, Bath, Monday, May 11, 1801
- Lyme Regis, Thursday, September 13, 1804
- Dolphin Inn assembly, Southampton, Tuesday, December 6, 1808
- Queen's Birthday Assembly Ball, Southampton, Wednesday, January 18, 1809
- A little dance, Chawton cottage, Thursday, April 16, 1812
- Concert and assembly, Saffery's Rooms, Canterbury, Friday, November 5, 1813
- Canterbury assembly, Thursday, November 11, 1813

THE MUSICIANS' GALLERY

POSSIBLE SUITORS

"To a question 'which of your characters do you like best?' she once answered 'Edmund Bertram and Mr. Knightley; but they are very far from being what I know English gentlemen often are.'"

—MRS. ANN BARRETT

◆ Tom Lefroy (see *Who Broke Her Heart*)

"After I had written the above, we received a visit from Mr Tom Lefroy and his cousin George. The latter is very well-behaved now; and as for the other, he has but <u>one</u> fault, which time will, I trust, entirely remove—it is that his morning coat is a great deal too light. He is a very great admirer of Tom Jones, and therefore wears the same coloured clothes, I imagine, which <u>he</u> did when he was wounded."

—JANE TO CASSANDRA, JANUARY 9, 1796

◆ Charles Watkins   ◆ John Lyford

"I danced twice with Warren last night, and once with Mr. Charles Watkins, and, to my inexpressible astonishment, I entirely escaped John Lyford. I was forced to fight hard for it, however."

—JANE TO CASSANDRA, JANUARY 9, 1796

◆ Mr. Heartly   ◆ Charles Powlett

"Tell Mary that I make over Mr Heartley & all his estate to her for her sole use and Benefit in future, & not only him, but all my other Admirers into the bargain wherever she can find them, even the kiss which C. Powlett wanted to give me, as I mean to confine myself in future to Mr. Tom Lefroy, for whom I do not care sixpence."

—JANE TO CASSANDRA, JANUARY 14, 1796

+ John Willing Warren

"Assure her also, as a last & indubitable proof of Warren's indifference to me, that he actually drew that Gentleman's picture for me, & delivered it to me without a Sigh."

—JANE TO CASSANDRA, JANUARY 14, 1796

+ Edward Taylor

"We went by Bifrons, & I contemplated with a melancholy pleasure, the abode of Him on whom I once fondly doated."

—JANE TO CASSANDRA, SEPTEMBER 15, 1796

+ Benjamin Portal

"Benjamin Portal is here. How charming that is!—I do not exactly know why, but the phrase followed so naturally that I could not help putting it down.— My mother saw him the other day, but without making herself known to him."

—JANE TO CASSANDRA, JUNE 11, 1799

+ Harris Bigg-Wither (see *The Hearts She Broke*)

"Harris still seems in a poor way, from his bad habit of body; his hand bled again a little the other day, & Dr Littlehales has been with him lately."

—JANE TO CASSANDRA, NOVEMBER 8, 1800

+ "An unnamed gentleman" from Devonshire

"When they were by the sea—I think she said in Devonshire; I don't think she named the place, and I am sure she did not say Lyme, for that I should have remembered—that he seemed greatly attracted by my Aunt Jane—I suppose it was an intercourse of some weeks—and that when they had to part (I imagine he was a visitor also, but his family might have lived near) he was urgent to know where they would be the next summer, implying or perhaps saying that he

should be there also, wherever it might be. I can only say that the impression left on Aunt Cassandra was that he had fallen in love with her sister, and was quite in earnest. Soon afterwards they heard of his death....I am sure she thought he was worthy of her sister, from the way in which she recalled his memory, and also that she did not doubt, either, that he would have been a successful suitor."

— NIECE CAROLINE AUSTEN RECORDING A REMINISCENCE SHE
HEARD FROM CASSANDRA SOMETIME BETWEEN 1801 AND 1804.

    ◆ William Digweed

"On Friday I wound up my four days of dissipation by meeting William Digweed at Deane, and am pretty well, I thank you, after it."

— JANE TO CASSANDRA, JANUARY 25, 1801

    ◆ Mr. Crawford   ◆ An "odd looking man"
    ◆ Mr. Granville   in Lyme

"Nobody asked me the first two dances—the two next I danced with Mr Crawford—& had I chosen to stay longer might have danced with Mr Granville, Mrs Granville's son—whom My dear friend Miss Armstrong offered to introduce to me—or with a new, odd looking man who had been eyeing me for some time, & at last without any introduction asked me if I meant to dance again.—I think he must be Irish by his ease, & because I imagine him to belong to the Honble Barnwalls, who are the son & son's wife of an Irish Viscount— bold, queerlooking people, just fit to be Quality at Lyme."

— JANE TO CASSANDRA, SEPTEMBER 14, 1804

    ◆ Edward Bridges (see *The Hearts She Broke*)

"We were agreeably surprised by Edward Bridges's company to it. He had been, strange to tell, too late for the cricket match, too late at least to play himself, and, not being asked to dine with the players, came home. It is impossible to

do justice to the hospitality of his attentions towards me; he made a point of ordering toasted cheese for supper entirely on my account."

—JANE TO CASSANDRA, AUGUST 27, 1805

   ✦   Mr. Papillon

"I am very much obliged to Mrs Knight for such a proof of the interest she takes in me—& she may depend upon it that I <u>will</u> marry Mr Papillon, whatever may be his reluctance or my own.—I owe her much more than such a trifling sacrifice."

—JANE TO CASSANDRA, DECEMBER 9, 1808

   ✦   Wyndham Knatchbull, Edward Knight's brother-in-law

"I depended upon hearing something of the Eveng from Mr W.K.,—& am very well satisfied with his notice of me—'A pleasing looking young woman';—that must do;—one cannot pretend to anything better now—thankful to have it continued a few years longer!"

—JANE TO CASSANDRA, APRIL 30, 1811

   ✦   Samuel Blackall

"He was a piece of Perfection, noisy Perfection himself which I always recollect with regard."

—JANE TO FRANK AUSTEN, JULY 3, 1813

   ✦   William Seymour, Henry Austen's lawyer and agent for Jane's books

"Henry is not quite well—a bilious attack with fever—he came back early from H. St yesterday & went to bed—the comical consequence of which was that Mr Seymour & I dined tete a tete."

—JANE TO CASSANDRA, OCTOBER 17, 1815

WHO BROKE HER HEART

Tom Lefroy

◆ Tom Lefroy

"You scold me so much in the nice long letter which I have this moment received from you, that I am almost afraid to tell you how my Irish friend and I behaved. Imagine to yourself everything most profligate and shocking in the way of dancing and sitting down together. I <u>can</u> expose myself however, only <u>once more</u>, because he leaves the country soon after next Friday, on which day we <u>are</u> to have a dance at Ashe after all. He is a very gentlemanlike, good-looking, pleasant young man, I assure you. But as to our having ever met, except at the three last balls, I cannot say much; for he is so excessively laughed at about me at Ashe, that he is ashamed of coming to Steventon, and ran away when we called on Mrs. Lefroy a few days ago."

—JANE TO CASSANDRA, JANUARY 9, 1796

· The next Friday:

"At length the Day is come on which I am to flirt my last with Tom Lefroy, & when you receive this it will be over—My tears flow as I write, at the melancholy idea."

—JANE TO CASSANDRA, JANUARY 15, 1796

· Three years later in a letter to Cassandra she confides:

"Mrs. Lefroy did come last Wednesday, and the Harwoods came likewise, but very considerately paid their visit before Mrs. Lefroy's arrival, with whom, in spite of interruptions both from my father and James, I was enough alone to hear all that was interesting, which you will easily credit when I tell you that of her nephew *she said nothing at all, and of her friend very little. She did not once mention the name of the former to <u>me</u>, and I was too proud to make any enquiries; but on my father's afterwards asking where he was, I learnt that he was gone back to London in his way to Ireland, where he is called to the Bar and means to practise."*

—JANE TO CASSANDRA, NOVEMBER 17, 1798

THE HEARTS SHE BROKE

✦ Harris Bigg-Wither

"Mr. Wither was very plain in person—awkward, & even uncouth in manner— nothing but his size to recommend him—he was a fine big man—but one need not look about for a secret reason to account for a young lady's <u>not</u> loving him—a great many would have taken him <u>without</u> love—& I beleive the wife he did get was very fond of him, & that they were a happy couple—He had sense in plenty & went through life very respectably, as a country gentleman—I <u>conjecture</u> that the advantages he could offer, & her gratitude for his love, & her long friendship with his family, induced my Aunt to decide that she would marry him <u>when</u> he should ask her—but that having accepted him she found she was miserable & that the place & fortune which would certainly be <u>his</u>, could not alter the <u>man</u>—She was staying in his <u>Father's</u> house—old Mr. Wither was then alive—To be sure she should not have said yes—over night—but I have always respected her for the courage in cancelling that yes—the next morning—All worldly advantages would have been to her—& she was of an age to know <u>this</u> quite well—My Aunts had very small fortunes & on their Father's death they & their Mother would be, they were aware, but poorly off—I beleive most young women so circumstanced would have taken Mr. W. & trusted to love after marriage."

—MARY LLOYD AUSTEN AS TOLD TO HER DAUGHTER CAROLINE AUSTEN

   ✦   Edward Bridges

"I wish you may be able to accept Lady Bridges's invitation, tho' I could not her son Edward's."

—JANE TO CASSANDRA, OCTOBER 7, 1808

HER CHORES

"I am very fond of experimental housekeeping, such as having an ox-cheek now and then; I shall have one next week, and I mean to have some little dumplings put into it, that I may fancy myself at Godmersham."

✦ Breakfast maker	✦ Sugar keeper
✦ Tea keeper	✦ Wine keeper

"At 9 o'clock she made breakfast—that was her part of the household work— The tea and sugar stores were under her charge—and the wine—Aunt Cassandra did all the rest."

—NIECE CAROLINE AUSTEN

HOUSEHOLD HELP

   ✦   James Elton

   ✦   Nanny Hilliard

"Our dinner was very good yesterday, & the Chicken boiled perfectly tender; therefore I shall not be obliged to dismiss Nanny on that account.—Almost every thing was unpacked & put away last night;—Nanny chose to do it, & I was not sorry to be busy."

- Nanny Littlewart

"You and Edward will be amused, I think, when you know that Nanny Littlewart dresses my hair."

- Molly
- John Bond

"John Bond begins to find himself grow old, which John Bonds ought not to do, and unequal to much hard work; a man is therefore hired to supply his place as to labour, and John himself is to have the care of the sheep."

- Phebe
- Turner
- Sally

"Sally knows your kind intentions & has received your message, & in return for it all, she & I have between us made out that she sends her Duty & thanks you for your goodness & means to be a good girl if I please."

- James
- Jenny
- Anne
- Isaac
- Mr. Choles

"We have been obliged to turn away Cholles, he grew so very drunken & negligent, & we have a Man in his place called Thomas."

- Mrs. Hall
- Mrs. Day
- Eliza
- Lyddy

- Thomas Carter
- Betsy
- Browning
- William

EDUCATION AND SCHOOLING

- Mrs. Cawley, boarding school, Oxford, age 7, March 1783
- Mrs. Cawley, boarding school moves to Southampton summer 1783
- Jane and Cassandra both became ill and return home to be schooled September 1783 because of typhus epidemic
- Watercolor lessons from artist John Claude Nattes, 1784
- The Abbey School, Mrs. La Tournelle's (Sarah Hackitt's) boarding school, Reading, 1785–1786

EARNINGS

- After the death of Mr. Austen, Mrs. Austen received £210 a year from her inheritance and that of daughter Cassandra from her deceased fiancé
- Annual gifts from her sons James, Henry, Edward, and Frank, which totaled £250
- Annual income of the three Chawton women was £460
- When Martha Lloyd joined them, she added her small income to their resources
- From Mrs. Lillingston, a friend of the Leigh-Perrots, £50

- Jane Austen invested £600 earned from her writing which yielded £30
- From four novels published in her lifetime, £684 13s

"As I find on looking into my affairs, that instead of being very rich I am likely to be very poor, I cannot afford more than ten shillings for Sackree; but as we are to meet in Canterbury I need not have mentioned this.——It is as well however, to prepare you for the sight of a Sister sunk in poverty, that it may not overcome your Spirits."

KINGS/RULERS WHEN SHE WAS ALIVE

- George III (active reign 1760–1811 [d. 1820])
- Prince Regent (regent 1811–1820; later George IV)

WARS DURING HER LIFE

- 1775–1783 American Revolutionary War
- 1792–1802 French Revolutionary Wars
- 1802 Treaty of Amiens ending France's war with Great Britain
- 1803 Napoleon breaks the Peace of Amiens and war begins again between Great Britain and France
- 1803–1815 Napoleonic Wars
- 1808–1814 Peninsular War
- 1812–1815 War of 1812
- 1814 Napoleon abdicates
- 1815 Battle of Waterloo; Napoleon defeated again

Her Correspondence

> "Her handwriting remains to bear testimony to its own excellence; and every note and letter of hers, was finished off handsomely—There was an art <u>then</u> in folding and sealing—no adhesive envelopes made all easy—some people's letters looked always loose and untidy—but her paper was sure to take the right folds, and <u>her</u> sealing wax to drop in the proper place."
>
> —CAROLINE AUSTEN

Several thousand were written, but only these survive, as far as we know. Here are the first two lines of a letter from each time Jane Austen changed her location.

♦ January 9–10, 1796
  · To Cassandra
  · Written from Steventon to Kintbury, Newbury

"In the first place I hope you will live twenty-three years longer. Mr. Tom Lefroy's birthday was yesterday, so that you are very near of an age."

♦ August 23, 1796
  · To Cassandra
  · Written from Cork Street, London

"Here I am once more in the Scene of Dissipation & vice, and I begin already to find my Morals corrupted.——We reached Staines yesterday I do not know when, without suffering so much from the Heat as I had hoped to do."

* September 1, 1796
  · To Cassandra
  · Written from Rowling to Steventon

"The letter which I have this moment received from you has diverted me beyond moderation. I could die of laughter at it, as they used to say at school."

* April 8, 1798
  · To Philadelphia Walter
  · Written from Steventon to Seal, Sevenoaks

"As Cassandra is at present from home, You must accept from my pen, our sincere Condolance on the melancholy Event which Mrs Humphries Letter announced to my Father this morning.——The loss of so kind & affectionate a Parent, must be a very severe affliction to all his Children, to yourself more especially, as your constant residence with him has given you so much the more constant & intimate Knowledge of his Virtues."

* October 24, 1798
  · To Cassandra
  · Written at the Bull and George, an inn in Dartford, to
    Godmersham, Faversham

"You have already heard from Daniel, I conclude, in what excellent time we reached and quitted Sittingbourne, and how very well my mother bore her journey thither. I am now able to send you a continuation of the same good account of her."

- ### October 27–28, 1798
  - To Cassandra
  - Written from Steventon to Godmersham

"Your letter was a most agreable surprize to me to day, & I have taken a long sheet of paper to shew my Gratitude. We arrived here yesterday between 4 & 5, but I cannot send you quite so triumphant an account of our last day's Journey as of the first & second."

- ### May 17, 1799
  - To Cassandra
  - Written at 13 Queen Square, Bath, to Steventon

"Our Journey yesterday went off exceedingly well; nothing occurred to alarm or delay us;—We found the roads in excellent order, had very good horses all the way, & reached Devizes with ease by 4 o'clock.—I suppose John has told you in what manner we were divided when we left Andover, & no alteration was afterwards made."

- ### October 25–27, 1800
  - To Cassandra
  - Written from Steventon to Godmersham

"I am not yet able to acknowledge the receipt of any parcel from London, which I suppose will not occasion you much surprise.—I was a little disappointed to day, but not more than is perfectly agreable; & I hope to be disappointed again tomorrow, as only one coach comes down on sundays."

- ### November 30–December 1, 1800
  - To Cassandra
  - Written from Ibthorpe, Manydown, to Godmersham

"Shall you expect to hear from me on Wednesday or not?—I think you will, or I

should not write, as the three days & half which have passed since my last letter was sent, have not produced many materials towards filling another sheet of paper."

❖ January 3–5, 1801
- · To Cassandra
- · Written from Steventon to Godmersham

"As you have by this time received my last letter, it is fit that I should begin another; & I begin with the hope, which is at present uppermost in my mind, that you often wore a white gown in the morning, at the time of all the gay party's being with you. Our visit at Ash Park last Wednesday, went off in a come-cá way; we met Mr Lefroy & Tom Chute, played at cards & came home again."

❖ February 11, 1801
- · To Cassandra
- · Written from Manydown to 24 Upper Berkeley Street, Portman Square, London

"As I have no Mr Smithson to write of I can date my letters.—Yours to my Mother has been forwarded to me this morning, with a request that I would take on me the office of acknowledging it."

❖ May 5–6, 1801
- · To Cassandra
- · Written from Paragon, Bath, to (Ibthorpe) Up Hurstbourne, Andover

"I have the pleasure of writing from my <u>own</u> room up two pair of stairs, with everything very comfortable about me. Our Journey here was perfectly free from accident or Event; we changed Horses at the end of every stage, & paid at almost every Turnpike;—we had charming weather, hardly any Dust, & were exceedingly agreable, as we did not speak above once in three miles."

◆ September 14, 1804

· To Cassandra

· Written from Lyme to (Ibthorpe) Hurstbourn Tarrant, Andover

"I take the first sheet of this fine striped paper to thank you for your letter from Weymouth, & express my hopes of your being at Ibthrop before this time. I expect to hear that you reached it yesterday Evening, being able to get as far as Blandford on wednesday."

◆ January 21, 1805

· To Frank Austen

· Written from Green Park Buildings, Bath, to HMS *Leopard*, Portsmouth

"I have melancholy news to relate, & sincerely feel for your feelings under the shock of it.——I wish I could better prepare You for it."

◆ April 8–11, 1805

· To Cassandra

· Written from 25 Gay Street, Bath, to Ibthorpe

"Here is a day for you! Did Bath or Ibthrop ever see a finer 8th of April?——It is March & April together, the glare of one & the warmth of the other."

◆ August 24, 1805

· To Cassandra

· Written from Godmersham to Goodnestone Farm, Wingham

"How do you do? & how is Harriot's cold?——I hope you are at this time sitting down to answer these questions."

◆ August 27, 1805

· To Cassandra

· Written from Goodnestone Farm to Godmersham

"We had a very pleasant drive from Canterbury, and reached this place about half-past four, which seemed to bid fair for a punctual dinner at five; but scenes of great agitation awaited us, and there was much to be endured and done before we could sit down to the table. Harriot found a letter from Louisa Hatton, desiring to know if she and her brothers were to be at the ball at Deal on Friday, and saying that the Eastwell family had some idea of going to it, and were to make use of Rowling if they did; and while I was dressing she came to me with another letter in her hand, in great perplexity."

⬩ July 1806
- · To Fanny Austen
- · Written from Clifton or Adlestrop to Godmersham

See they come, post haste from Thanet,
Lovely couple; side by side;
They've left behind them Richard Kennet
With the Parents of the Bride!

⬩ January 7–8, 1807
- · To Cassandra
- · Written from Southampton to Godmersham

"You were mistaken in supposing I should expect your letter on Sunday; I had no idea of hearing from you before Tuesday, and my pleasure yesterday was therefore unhurt by any previous disappointment. I thank you for writing so much; you must really have sent me the value of two letters in one."

⬩ June 15–17, 1808
- · To Cassandra

· Written from Godmersham to Castle Square, Southampton

"Where shall I begin? Which of all my important nothings shall I tell you first?"

❖ October 1–2, 1808
· To Cassandra
· Written from Castle Square, Southampton, to Godmersham

"Your letter this morning was quite unexpected, & it is well that it brings such good news to counterbalance the disappointment to me of losing my first sentence, which I had arranged full of proper hopes about your Journey, intending to commit them to paper to day, & not looking for certainty till tomorrow.——We are extremely glad to hear of the birth of the Child, & trust everything will proceed as well as it begins;—his Mama has our best wishes, & he our second best for health & comfort—tho' I suppose unless <u>he</u> has our best too, we do nothing for <u>her</u>."

❖ July 26, 1809
· To Frank Austen
· Written from Chawton to China

My dearest Frank, I wish you joy
Of Mary's safety with a Boy,
Whose birth has given little pain
Compared with that of Mary Jane.——
May he a growing Blessing prove,
And well deserve his Parents' Love!

❖ April 18–20, 1811
· To Cassandra
· Written from Sloane Street, London, to Godmersham

"I have so many matters to tell you of, that I cannot wait any longer before I begin to put them down.—I spent tuesday in Bentinck St, the Cookes called here & took me back; & it was quite a Cooke day, for the Miss Rolles paid a visit while I was there, & Sam Arnold dropt in to tea."

* May 29, 1811
  · To Cassandra
  · Written from Chawton to Godmersham

"It was a mistake of mine, my dear Cassandra, to talk of a 10th Child at Hamstall; I had forgot there were but 8 already.—Your enquiry after my Uncle & Aunt were most happily timed, for the very same post brought an account of them."

* May 20, 1813
  · To Cassandra
  · Written from Sloane Street, London, to Chawton

"Before I say anything else, I claim a paper full of Halfpence on the Drawingroom Mantlepeice; I put them there myself & forgot to bring them with me.—I cannot say that I have yet been in any distress for Money, but I chuse to have my due as well as the Devil."

* July 3–6, 1813
  · To Frank Austen
  · Written from Chawton to HMS *Elephant*, the Baltic Sea

"Behold me going to write you as handsome a Letter as I can. Wish me good luck."

* September 15–16, 1813
  · To Cassandra
  · Written from Henrietta Street, London, to Chawton

"Here I am, my dearest Cassandra, seated in the Breakfast, Dining, sitting room,

*beginning with all my might. Fanny will join me as soon as she is dressed &
begin her Letter."*

> ✦ September 23–24, 1813
> > · To Cassandra
> > · Written from Godmersham to Chawton

*"Thank you five hundred & forty times for the exquisite peice of Workmanship
which was brought into the room this morng, while we were at breakfast—with
some very inferior works of art in the same way, & which I read with high
glee—much delighted with everything it told whether good or bad."*

> ✦ March 2–3, 1814
> > · To Cassandra
> > · Written from Henrietta Street, London, to Chawton

*"You were wrong in thinking of us at Guildford last night, we were at Cobham.
On reaching G. we found that John & the Horses were gone on."*

> ✦ June 14, 1814
> > · To Cassandra
> > · Written from Chawton to 10 Henrietta Street, London

*"Fanny takes my Mother to Alton this morng which gives me an opportunity of
sending you a few lines, without any other trouble than that of writing them. This
is a delightful day in the Country, & I hope not much too hot for Town."*

> ✦ August 23–24, 1814
> > · To Cassandra
> > · Written from 23 Hans Place, London, to Chawton

*"I had a very good Journey, not crouded, two of the three taken up at Bentley
being Children, the others of a reasonable size; & they were all very quiet &*

civil.——*We were late in London, from being a great Load & from changing Coaches at Farnham, it was nearly 4 I believe when we reached Sloane St; Henry himself met me, & as soon as my Trunk & Basket could be routed out from all the other Trunks & Baskets in the World, we were on our way to Hans Place in the Luxury of a nice large cool dirty Hackney Coach."*

- ◆ September 9–18, 1814
  - · To Anna Austen
  - · Written from Chawton to Steventon

"We have been very much amused by your 3 books, but I have a good many criticisms to make—more than you will like. We are not satisfied with Mrs F.'s settling herself as Tenant & near Neighbour to such a Man as Sir T.H. without having some other inducement to go there; she ought to have some friend living thereabouts to tempt her."

- ◆ November 29, 1814
  - · To Anna Lefroy
  - · Written from 23 Hans Place, London, to Hendon

"I am very much obliged to you, my dear Anna, & should be very happy to come & see you again if I could, but I have not a day disengaged. We are expecting your Uncle Charles tomorrow; and I am to go the next day to Hanwell to fetch some Miss Moores who are to stay here till Saturday; then comes Sunday & Elizth Gibson, and on Monday Your Uncle Henry takes us both to Chawton."

- ◆ December 1814
  - · To Caroline Austen
  - · Written from Chawton to Steventon

"I wish I could finish Stories as fast as you can.——I am much obliged to you for the sight of Olivia, & think you have done for her very well; but the good for

nothing Father, who was the real author of all her Faults & Sufferings, should not escape unpunished."

    ✦ October 17–18, 1815
      · To Cassandra
      · Written from 23 Hans Place, London, to Chawton

"Thank you for your two Letters. I am very glad the new Cook begins so well."

    ✦ December 31, 1815
      · To Countess of Morley
      · Written from Chawton to Saltram

"Accept my Thanks for the honour of your note & for your kind Disposition in favour of Emma. In my present State of Doubt as to her reception in the World, it is particularly gratifying to me to receive so early an assurance of your Ladyship's approbation."

    ✦ May 27, 1817
      · To James Edward Austen
      · Written from College Street, Winchester, to Exeter College, Oxford

"I know no better way my dearest Edward, of thanking you for your most affectionate concern for me during my illness, than by telling you myself as soon as possible that I continue to get better.——I will not boast of my handwriting; neither that, nor my face have yet recovered their proper beauty, but in other respects I am gaining strength very fast."

Timeline of Jane's Life

1775 Jane is born in Steventon, Saturday, December 16.

1776 Public baptism is held in Steventon, Good Friday, April 5.

1781 Age 5, The Austens are visited in Steventon by Reverend Thomas Leigh of Adlestrop, Mrs. Austen's cousin, Tuesday, April 3.

1782 Age 6, Jane and her younger brother Charles run down the lane to greet their father and sister Cassandra on a return from a trip during the summer.

1783 Age 7, Jane moves to Oxford with Cassandra and their cousin Jane Cooper to be tutored by Mrs. Cawley in March. She returns to Steventon in the fall after an outbreak of typhus near the school, which had moved to Southampton.

1784 Age 8, The Austen children perform *The Rivals*, by Richard Brinsley Sheriden in July.

1785 Age 9, Austen girls and Jane Cooper start the school year at the Abbey House School in Reading, run by Mrs. La Tournelle, Monday, July 25.

1786 Age 11, Jane returns to Steventon to be schooled at home and arrives in time for a visit by Mr. Austen's sister Philadelphia Hancock, her daughter Eliza de Feuillide, and her young son, Hastings, in December.

1787 Age 12, *The Wonder: A Woman Keeps a Secret*, a comedy by Susannah Centlivre, is performed by Austen family and friends on December 26 and 28.

1788 Age 12, Jane's story *Henry and Eliza* is dedicated to cousin Jane Cooper sometime between December and January 1789.

1789 Age 13, Martha and Mary Lloyd move into the neighborhood in the spring.

1790 Age 14, Jane finishes writing *Love and Freindship*, a novel in a series of letters, on Sunday, June 13, with a dedication to Madame la Comtesse de Feuillide.

1791 Age 15, Jane finishes writing *The History of England* and dedicates it to sister Cassandra on Saturday, November 26.

1792 Age 16, In the autumn Jane makes her ball debut at Enham House in nearby Andover, home of the Dewars, relatives of the Mathews.

1793 Age 17, Jane completes her *Juvenilia*'s last composition, "Ode to Pity," Monday, June 3, dedicated to Cassandra.

1794 Age 18, Mr. Austen buys a "a Small Mahogany Writing Desk with 1 Long Drawer and Glass Ink Stand Compleat" for twelve shillings, likely the desk owned by Jane on Friday, December 5.

1795 Age 19, Jane's niece Anna, two years old, arrives at Steventon after older brother James's wife dies on May 3.

1796 Age 20, Tom Lefroy calls on Jane Saturday, the day after a nighttime ball where they danced together at nearby Manydown on Friday, January 8.

1797 Age 21, Jane finishes composing *First Impressions*, the original version of *Pride and Prejudice*, in August.

1798 Age 22, Jane, her mother, father, and sister arrive at her brother Edward's grand home, Godmersham, for the first time in late August.

1799 Age 23, Jane, her mother, and Edward, with his family and servants, travel to Bath to visit her aunt and uncle, the Leigh-Perrots, in mid-May.

1800 Age 24, Jane's parents inform her in early December they're leaving Steventon and moving to Bath.

1801 Age 25, Jane goes to a ball in Bath's Upper Rooms with the Leigh-Perrots Monday, May 11.

1802 Age 26, Harris Bigg-Wither proposes marriage on Thursday, December 2. Jane rescinds her acceptance the next day.

1803 Age 27, *Susan*, the first version of *Northanger Abbey*, is sold to Benjamin Crosby & Son for £10 in the spring.

1804 Age 28, While visiting Lyme Regis, Jane and a friend walk for an hour on the Cobb September 13.

1805 Age 29, Mr. Austen dies on Monday, January 21.

1806 Age 30, Mrs. Austen, Jane, Cassandra, and their friend Martha Lloyd leave Bath for good July 2, eventually arriving in Southampton, their new home, October 10.

1807 Age 31, Jane, her mother, and Cassandra visit brother Edward's Chawton House Tuesday, September 1.

1808 Age 32, On her birthday, Jane writes a poem in memory of Mrs. Lefroy, who died on the same date, December 16, four years earlier.

1809 Age 33, Jane, Cassandra, her mother, and Martha Lloyd move into Chawton Cottage Friday, July 7.

1810 Age 34, Thomas Egerton agrees during the winter to publish *Sense and Sensibility*.

1811 Age 35, Jane travels with her brother Henry to his London home on Sloane Street in the spring to correct proofs of *Sense and Sensibility*. It's published October 30.

"No indeed, I am never too busy to think of S&S. I can no more forget it than a mother can forget her sucking child, & I am much obliged to you for your enquiries."

1812 Age 36, In a letter written November 29 to Martha Lloyd, Jane writes "P. & P. is sold—Egerton gives £110 for it."

1813 Age 37, In London, Jane and Henry go to art exhibitions in Pall Mall in May.

1814 Age 38, Jane begins *Emma* January 21; *Mansfield Park* is published May 9.

1815 Age 39, On August 8, Jane begins *Persuasion*.

1816 Age 40, Jane writes James Stanier Clarke, Monday, December 11, acknowledging the Prince Regent's thanks for receiving a copy of *Emma*, which includes a dedication to him.

1817 Age 41, Jane moves to Winchester on Saturday, May 24, to be treated by Mr. Lyford at the Hampshire County Hospital. She died at dawn Friday, July 18, at 8 College Street, Winchester, with sister Cassandra by her side.

Her Writing

Everything she wrote that we know of

JUVENILIA

WRITTEN AGES 11 TO 17
(1787–93 OR 94)

- *Volume the First*
    - *Frederic & Elfrida**
    - *Jack & Alice*
    - *Edgar & Emma*
    - *Henry & Eliza*
    - *The Adventures of Mr. Harley*
    - *Sir William Mountague*
    - *Memoirs of Mr. Clifford*
    - *The Beautifull Cassandra*
    - *Amelia Webster*
    - *The Visit*
    - *The Mystery*
    - *The Three Sisters*
    - *A Beautiful Description*
    - *The Generous Curate*
    - *"Ode to Pity"***

*Chapter the First on page 194.
**First stanza on page 134.

- *Volume the Second*
  - · *Love and Freindship*
  - · *Lesley Castle*
  - · *The History of England*
  - · *A Collection of Letters*
  - · *The Female Philosopher*

  - · *The First Act of a Comedy*
  - · *A Letter from a Young Lady*
  - · *A Tour through Wales*
  - · *A Tale*

- *Volume the Third*
  - · *Evelyn*

  - · *Catharine, or the Bower*

- Other writings
  - · *Scraps*
  - · *"Miscellanious Morsels"*

  - · *Sir Charles Grandison or The Happy Man, a Comedy*

NOVELLA

- *Lady Susan*, age 17 to 19 (1793–1795; 1805–?)

JANE'S NOVELS

- *Sense and Sensibility*, originally *Elinor and Marianne*
  - · 1795: Jane begins *E&M*
  - · November 1797: book becomes *S&S*
  - · Winter of 1810: *S&S* finds a publisher
  - · October 30, 1811: published
- *Pride and Prejudice*, originally *First Impressions*
  - · October 1796: Jane begins *FI*

- August 1797: *FI* finished
- November 1, 1797: Mr. Austen sends *FI* to publisher Thomas Cadell. It's rejected by return post.
- Winter 1811: revision of *FI*
- January 28, 1813: published as *Pride and Prejudice*

◆ *Northanger Abbey*, originally *Susan*
  - Summer 1798: Jane begins *Susan*
  - Summer 1799: likely completes *Susan*
  - Late 1802 or early 1803: revises *Susan*
  - Spring 1803: sells *Susan* copyright to publisher Benjamin Crosby
  - Spring 1816: Henry buys back rights, Jane begins revision with new title, *Catherine*
  - December 1817: published as *Northanger Abbey*

◆ *Mansfield Park*
  - February 1811: Jane begins
  - July 1813: completes
  - November 1813: accepted by publisher Thomas Egerton
  - May 9, 1814: published by John Murray

◆ *Emma*
  - January 21, 1814: Jane begins
  - March 29, 1815: Jane finishes
  - December 1815: published

◆ *Persuasion*
  - August 8, 1815: Jane begins
  - August 6, 1816: Jane finishes
  - December 1817: published by John Murray, five months after her death

Unfinished Novels

- *The Watsons*
  - 1804

- *Sanditon*
  - January 27–March 18, 1817: works on *Sanditon*

Poetry She Wrote from Age Sixteen on, the First Stanza

This Little Bag
Written to Mary Lloyd and enclosed in small bag
with a little sewing kit, January 1792

This little bag I hope will prove
To be not vainly made—
For, if you thread & needle want
It will afford you aid.
And as we are about to part
'Twill serve another end,
For when you look upon the bag
You'll recollect your friend.

ODE TO PITY
June 3, 1793

1

Ever musing I delight to tread
The Paths of honour and the Myrtle Grove
Whilst the pale Moon her beams doth shed
On disappointed Love.
While Philomel on airy hawthorn Bush
Sings sweet and Melancholy, And the thrush
Converses with the Dove.

LINES SUPPOSED TO HAVE BEEN
SENT TO AN UNCIVIL DRESSMAKER
Written to Martha Lloyd after her mother died, spring 1805

Miss Lloyd has now sent to Miss Green,
As, on opening the box, may be seen,
Some yards of a Black Ploughman's Gauze,
To be made up directly, because
Miss Lloyd must in mourning appear—
For the death of a Relative dear—
Miss Lloyd must expect to receive
This license to mourn & to grieve,
Complete, er'e the end of the week—
It is better to write than to speak—

OH! MR BEST
On Leaving Bath, July 1806, Clifton

Oh! Mr Best, you're very bad
And all the world shall know it;
Your base behaviour shall be sung
By me, a tuneful Poet.—

LINES WRITTEN BY JANE AUSTEN FOR THE AMUSEMENT OF A NIECE
On the marriage of Frank Austen and Mary Gibson, July 1806

See they come, post haste from Thanet,
Lovely couple, side by side;
They've left behind them Richard Kennet
With the Parents of the Bride!

ON SIR HOME POPHAM'S SENTENCE
April 1807

Of a Ministry pitiful, angry, mean,
A Gallant Commander the victim is seen;
For Promptitude, Vigour, Success, does he stand
Condemn'd to receive a severe reprimand!
To his Foes I could wish a resemblance in fate;
That they too may suffer themselves soon or late
The Injustice they warrant—but vain is my Spite,
They cannot so suffer, who never do right.

VERSES TO RHYME WITH *ROSE*
September 1807

Happy the Lab'rer in his Sunday Cloathes!—
In light-drab coat, smart waistcoat, well-darn'd Hose
And hat upon his head, to Church he goes;—
As oft with conscious pride, he downward throws
A glance upon the ample Cabbage rose
Which, stuck in Buttonhole, regales his nose,
He envies not the gayest London beaux.—
In Church he takes his seat among the rows,
Pays to the Place the reverence he owes,
Likes best the Prayers whose meaning least he knows,
Lists to the Sermon in a softening Doze,
And rouses joyous at the welcome close.

TO MISS BIGG
Verse included with pocket handkerchiefs Jane embroidered for Catherine
Bigg on her marriage to Reverend Herbert Hill, August 26, 1808

Cambrick! with grateful blessings would I pay
The pleasure given me in sweet employ;
Long may'st thou serve my friend without decay,
And have no Tears to wipe, but Tears of joy!

The version she didn't send:

Cambrick! Thou'st been to me a Good,
And I would bless thee if I could.
Go, serve thy Mistress with delight,
Be small in compass, soft & white;
Enjoy thy fortune, honour'd much
To bear her name and feel her touch;
And that thy worth may last for years,
Slight be her Colds, & few her Tears.

TO THE MEMORY OF MRS. LEFROY
WHO DIED DEC:R 16—MY BIRTHDAY
1808

The day returns again, my natal day;
What mix'd emotions with the Thought arise!
Beloved friend, four years have pass'd away
Since thou wert snatch'd forever from our eyes.

ALAS! POOR BRAG
In a letter to Cassandra from Castle Square to Godmersham,
January 17, 1809

"Alas! poor Brag, thou boastful Game!
What now avails thine empty name?—
Where now thy more distinguish'd fame—
My day is o'er, & Thine the same.—

For thou like me art thrown aside,
At Godmersham, this Christmas Tide;
And now across the Table wide, Each
Game save Brag or Spec: is tried.——"
"Such is the mild Ejaculation,
Of tender hearted Speculation."

MY DEAREST FRANK

Commemorating the birth of brother Frank's first son, July 26, 1809

My dearest Frank, I wish you joy
Of Mary's safety with a boy,
Whose birth has given little pain,
Compared with that of Mary Jane.
May he a growing Blessing prove,
And well deserve his Parents' Love!
Endow'd with Art's & Nature's Good,
Thy name possessing with thy Blood;
In him, in all his ways, may we
Another Francis William see!——
Thy infant days may he inherit,
Thy warmth, nay insolence of spirit;——
We would not with one fault dispense
To weaken the resemblance.
May he revive thy Nursery sin,
Peeping as daringly within,
(His curley Locks but just descried)
With "Bet, my be not come to bide."

IN MEASURED VERSE

A Poem for Anna Lefroy, Jane's Niece, summer 1810

In measured verse I'll now rehearse
The charms of lovely Anna:
And, first, her mind is unconfined
Like any vast savannah.

I'VE A PAIN IN MY HEAD

Lines on Maria Beckford, February 7, 1811

"I've a pain in my head"
Said the suffering Beckford;
To her Doctor so dread.
"Ah! what shall I take for't?"

I AM IN A DILEMMA

In a letter to Cassandra, April 30, 1811, from Sloane Street, London

"I am in a Dilemma, for want of an Emma,"
"Escaped from the Lips, Of Henry Gipps."

Between Session & Session
Poetry for Edward and his Daughter
In a Letter to Cassandra, April 30, 1811

"Between Session & Session"
"The first Prepossession"
"May rouse up the Nation"
"And the Villianous Bill"
"May be forced to lie Still"
"Against Wicked Men's will."

On the Marriage of Mr Gell of East Bourn to Miss Gill
1811

Of Eastbourn, Mr Gell
From being perfectly well
Became dreadfully ill
For the love of Miss Gill.

When Stretch'd on One's Bed
October 27, 1811

When stretch'd on one's bed
With a fierce-throbbing head
Which precludes alike Thought or Repose,
How little one cares
For the grandest affairs
That may busy the world as it goes!—

ON THE MARRIAGE OF MISS CAMILLA
WALLOP & THE REV'D WAKE

Married March 26, 1813

Camilla, good humoured, & merry, & small
For a Husband was at her last stake;
And having in vain danced at many a Ball
Is now happy to jump at a Wake.

ST. SWITHIN'S DAY*

HER PRAYERS,
FIRST THREE SENTENCES

"Prayers Composed by my ever dear
Sister Jane"—Cassandra

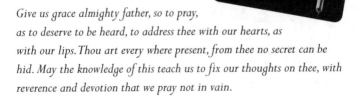

1

Give us grace almighty father, so to pray,
as to deserve to be heard, to address thee with our hearts, as
with our lips. Thou art every where present, from thee no secret can be
hid. May the knowledge of this teach us to fix our thoughts on thee, with
reverence and devotion that we pray not in vain.

*See *Her Last Work*, page 196

2

Almighty God! Look down with mercy on thy servants here assembled and accept the petitions now offered up unto thee. Pardon oh! God the offences of the past day. We are conscious of many frailties; we remember with shame and contrition, many evil thoughts and neglected duties; and we have perhaps sinned against thee and against our fellow-creatures in many instances of which we have no remembrance.

3

Father of Heaven! whose goodness has brought us in safety to the close of this day, dispose our hearts in fervent prayer. Another day is now gone, and added to those, for which we were before accountable. Teach us almighty father, to consider this solemn truth, as we should do, that we may feel the importance of every day, and every hour as it passes, and earnestly strive to make a better use of what thy goodness may yet bestow on us, than we have done of the time past.

OPENING LINES OF HER NOVELS AND NOVELLA

♦ *Sense and Sensibility*

"The family of Dashwood had long been settled in Sussex."

♦ *Pride and Prejudice*

"It is a truth universally acknowledged, that a single man in possession of a good fortune, must be in want of a wife."

Mansfield Park

"About thirty years ago, Miss Maria Ward, of Huntingdon, with only seven thousand pounds, had the good luck to captivate Sir Thomas Bertram, of Mansfield Park, in the county of Northampton, and to be thereby raised to the rank of baronet's lady, with all the comforts and consequences of an handsome house and large income."

Emma

"Emma Woodhouse, handsome, clever, and rich, with a comfortable home and happy disposition, seemed to unite some of the best blessings of existence; and had lived nearly twenty-one years in the world with very little to distress or vex her."

Northanger Abbey

"No one who had ever seen Catherine Morland in her infancy, would have supposed her born to be an heroine."

Persuasion

"Sir Walter Elliot, of Kellynch-hall, in Somersetshire, was a man who, for his own amusement, never took up any book but the Baronetage; there he found occupation for an idle hour, and consolation in a distressed one; there his faculties were roused into admiration and respect, by contemplating the limited remnant of the earliest patents; there any unwelcome sensations, arising from domestic affairs, changed naturally into pity and contempt, as he turned over the almost endless creations of the last century—and there, if every other leaf were powerless, he could read his own history with an interest which never failed—this was the page at which the favourite volume was always opened: ELLIOT OF KELLYNCH HALL."

* *Lady Susan*

"MY DEAR BROTHER,—I can no longer refuse myself the pleasure of profiting by your kind invitation when we last parted of spending some weeks with you at Churchill, and, therefore, if quite convenient to you and Mrs. Vernon to receive me at present, I shall hope within a few days to be introduced to a sister whom I have so long desired to be acquainted with."

MIDPOINTS

* *Sense and Sensibility*

"It is too much! Oh! Willoughby, Willoughby, could this be yours! Cruel, cruel—nothing can acquit you."

* *Pride and Prejudice*

"You have said quite enough, madam. I perfectly comprehend your feelings, and have now only to be ashamed of what my own have been. Forgive me for having taken up so much of your time, and accept my best wishes for your health and happiness."

* *Mansfield Park*

"It was a picture which Henry Crawford had moral taste enough to value. Fanny's attractions increased—increased two-fold—for the sensibility which beautified her complexion and illumined her countenance, was an attraction in itself. He was no longer in doubt of the capabilities of her heart. She had feeling, genuine feeling."

◆ *Emma*

"Well, I am so sorry!—Oh! Mr. Knightley, what a delightful party last night; how extremely pleasant.—Did you ever see such dancing?—Was not it delightful?—Miss Woodhouse and Mr. Frank Churchill; I never saw anything equal to it."

◆ *Northanger Abbey*

"But as for General Tilney, I assure you it would be impossible for anybody to behave to me with greater civility and attention; it seemed to be his only care to entertain and make me happy."

◆ *Persuasion*

"Don't talk of it, don't talk of it," he cried. "Oh God! that I had not given way to her at the fatal moment! Had I done as I ought! But so eager and so resolute! Dear, sweet Louisa!"

◆ *Lady Susan*

"Such earnestness such solemnity of expression! and yet I cannot help suspecting the truth of everything she says."

SPOILER ALERT! LAST LINES

◆ *Sense and Sensibility*

"Between Barton and Delaford, there was that constant communication which strong family affection would naturally dictate;—and among the merits and the happiness of Elinor and Marianne, let it not be ranked as the least considerable, that though sisters, and living almost within sight of each other, *they could live without disagreement between themselves, or producing coolness between their husbands."*

* *Pride and Prejudice*

"Darcy, as well as Elizabeth, really loved them [the Gardiners]; and they were both ever sensible of the warmest gratitude towards the persons who, by bringing her into Derbyshire, had been the means of uniting them."

* *Mansfield Park*

"On that event they removed to Mansfield, and the parsonage there, which under each of its two former owners, Fanny had never been able to approach but with some painful sensation of restraint or alarm, soon grew as dear to her heart, and as thoroughly perfect in her eyes, as every thing else within the view and patronage of Mansfield Park, had long been."

* *Emma*

"But, in spite of these deficiencies, the wishes, the hopes, the confidence, the predictions of the small band of true friends who witnessed the ceremony, were fully answered in the perfect happiness of the union."

* *Northanger Abbey*

"To begin perfect happiness at the respective ages of twenty-six and eighteen, is to do pretty well; and professing myself moreover convinced that the general's unjust interference, so far from being really injurious to their felicity, was perhaps rather conducive to it, by improving their knowledge of each other, and adding strength to their attachment, I leave it to be settled, by whomsoever it may concern, whether the tendency of this work be altogether to recommend parental tyranny, or reward filial disobedience."

◆ *Persuasion*

"She gloried in being a sailor's wife, but she must pay the tax of quick alarm, for belonging to that profession which is—if possible—more distinguished in its domestic virtues than in its national importance."

◆ *Lady Susan*

"For myself, I confess that I can pity only Miss Mainwaring; who, coming to town, and putting herself to an expense in clothes which impoverished her for two years, on purpose to secure him, was defrauded of her due by a woman ten years older than herself."

CHARACTERS IN THE NOVELS, IN ORDER OF APPEARANCE

◆ *Sense and Sensibility*

- Henry Dashwood, late husband of Mrs. Dashwood
- Harry Dashwood, son of John and Fanny
- Mrs. Dashwood, widow of Henry and mother of Dashwood sisters
- Elinor Dashwood, heroine, oldest
- Marianne Dashwood, heroine, middle
- Margaret Dashwood, youngest
- John Dashwood, Henry Dashwood's son from first marriage
- Fanny Dashwood, wife of John
- Edward Ferrars, Fanny Dashwood's brother
- Sir John Middleton, cousin of Mrs. Dashwood, owner of Barton Park
- Lady Mary Middleton, Sir John's wife
- John Middleton, eldest son of Sir John and Lady Middleton

- William Middleton, son of the Middletons

- Annamaria Middleton, daughter of the Middletons

- Mrs. Jennings, Lady Middleton's mother

- Colonel Brandon, neighbor of the Middletons

- John Willoughby, lives not far from Barton cottage

- Fanny Brandon, Colonel Brandon's cousin

- Eliza Williams, Colonel Brandon's ward

- The Misses Carey, Middleton neighbors

- Mrs. Smith, cousin and Willoughby's potential benefactor

- Whitakers, Middleton's neighbors

- Mrs. Ferrars, mother of Fanny, Edward, and Robert

- Charlotte Palmer, daughter of Mrs. Jennings

- Thomas Palmer, husband of Charlotte

- Gilberts, friends of the Middletons

- Westons, friends of the Palmers

- Lucy Steele, cousin of Mrs. Jennings

- Anne (Nancy) Steele, older sister of Lucy

- Mr. Rose, would-be beau of Anne Steele

- Mr. Simpson, Mr. Rose's employer

- Robert Ferrars, brother of Fanny and Edward

- Mr. Pratt, uncle of the Misses Steele, Edward's tutor

- Cartwright, Mrs. Jenning's household help

- Mrs. Taylor, friend of Mrs. Jennings

- Sophia Grey, Willoughby's betrothed, later wife

- Parrys, friends of Mrs. Jennings

- Sandersons, friends of Mrs. Jennings

- Biddy Henshawe, Miss Grey's aunt

- Miss Walker, friend of Mrs. Taylor

- Mr. and Mrs. Ellison, Miss Grey's guardians

- Mr. Brandon, Colonel Brandon's brother
- Eliza Williams, who later became Mrs. Brandon
- Dr. Davies, a potential beau of Anne Steele
- Honourable Miss Morton, Mrs. Ferrar's match for her son Edward
- Lord Morton, Miss Morton's father
- Gibson, former resident of East Kingham Farm
- Sir Robert Ferrars, Edward's uncle
- Lord Courtland, friend of Robert Ferrars
- Bonomi, architect in Jane Austen's lifetime
- Lady Elliott, friend of Robert Ferrars
- Mrs. Dennison, friend of John and Fanny Dashwood
- Mr. Donavan, healthcare professional
- Betty, maid of Mrs. Jennings
- Mrs. Clarke, friend of Mrs. Jennings
- Miss Godby, friend of Miss Sparks
- Miss Sparks, friend of Anne Steele
- Richard, cousin of Anne Steele
- Mrs. Richardson, friend of Anne Steele
- Martha Sharpe, friend of Anne Steele
- Mr. Steele, father of the Misses Steele
- Mr. Harris, Mrs. Palmer's doctor
- Thomas, Mrs. Dashwood's servant
- Sally, Middleton household servant
- Mrs. Burgess, friend of Anne Steele

- *Pride and Prejudice*
  - Mr. Bennet, father of the Bennet girls
  - Mrs. Bennet, mother of the Bennet girls
  - Mrs. Long, the Bennets' neighbor
  - Mr. Morris, arranged for Bingley to let Netherfield

- Charles Bingley, renter of Netherfield
- Sir William Lucas, the Bennets' neighbor
- Lady Lucas, Sir William's wife
- Elizabeth (Lizzy, Eliza) Bennet, heroine, second-oldest daughter of the Bennets
- Jane Bennet, eldest
- Lydia Bennet, fifth
- Catherine (Kitty) Bennet, fourth
- Mary Bennet, third
- Mr. Hurst, husband of Bingley's sister
- Mr. Darcy, Bingley's friend
- Louisa Hurst, Bingley's sister
- Caroline Bingley, Bingley's sister
- Charlotte Lucas, daughter of Sir William and Lady Lucas, friend of Elizabeth
- Mary King, wealthy neighbor
- Maria Lucas, younger sister of Charlotte
- Mr. Robinson, man at neighborhood assembly
- Colonel Forster, militia member stationed at Meryton
- Mr. Philips, Mrs. Bennet's brother-in-law
- Mrs. Philips, Mrs. Bennet's sister
- Captain Carter, militia member
- Miss Watson, Meryton resident
- Miss Grantley, acquaintance of Caroline Bingley
- Mr. Jones, local healthcare professional
- Edward Gardiner, Mrs. Bennet's brother
- Mrs. Nicholls, Bingley's cook
- Mr. William Collins, Mr. Bennet's cousin, Longbourn heir
- Right Honourable Lady Catherine de Bourgh, Darcy's aunt

- Sir Lewis de Bourgh, Lady Catherine's late husband
- Anne de Bourgh, Lady Catherine's daughter
- Richard, Phillips's servant
- Mr. Denny, soldier in the militia
- George Wickham, soldier in the militia, grew up with Darcy
- Mr. Wickham, father of George Wickham
- The late Mr. Darcy, Darcy's father
- Georgiana Darcy, Darcy's younger sister
- Lady Anne Darcy, Georgiana and Darcy's late mother
- Mrs. Jenkinson, Miss de Bourgh's companion
- Mrs. Gardiner, Mr. Gardiner's wife
- The Misses Webb, acquaintances of Catherine de Bourgh
- Lady Metcalfe, friend of Catherine de Bourgh
- Miss Pope, acquaintance of Lady Metcalfe
- Colonel Fitzwilliam, Darcy's cousin
- Mrs. Younge, Georgiana's caretaker
- Dawson, Lady Catherine's maid
- John, Collins's servant
- Harriet Forster, Colonel Forster's wife and Lydia's friend
- Harriet Harrington, friend of Lydia and Mrs. Forster

- Pen Harrington, Harriet's sister
- Chamberlayne, soldier in the militia
- Pratt, soldier in the militia
- Colonel Millar, member of the militia
- Mrs. Reynolds, housekeeper of Pemberley
- Mrs. Annesley, Georgiana's companion
- John, the Gardiners' servant

- Sally, Mrs. Forster's maid
- Mrs. Hill, housekeeper at Longbourn
- Haggerston, Mr. Gardiner's business associate
- William Goulding, resident of Haye Park
- Mr. Stone, Mr. Gardiner's business associate
- Gouldings, residents of Haye Park

Mansfield Park

- Maria Ward, Thomas Bertram's wife, Lady Bertram
- Sir Thomas Bertram, owner of Mansfield Park
- Mrs. (Miss Ward) Norris, older sister of Lady Bertram
- Mrs. Fanny (Frances Ward) Price, younger sister of Lady Bertram and Mrs. Norris
- Reverend Mr. Norris, late husband of Mr. Norris
- Mr. Price, Fanny Price's husband, lieutenant in the marines
- Tom Bertram, oldest Bertram son
- Edmund Bertram, other Bertram son
- Nanny, Mrs. Norris's servant
- Miss Lee, governess
- Ellis, maid
- Fanny Price, heroine, Bertram's niece
- Julia Bertram, younger Bertram daughter
- Maria Bertram, Julia's older sister
- William Price, lieutenant in the navy, Fanny's older brother
- Dr. Grant, rector of Mansfield
- Mrs. Grant, wife of Dr. Grant
- James Rushworth, fiancé, then husband, of Maria Bertram
- Henry Crawford, Mrs. Grant's half brother
- Mary Crawford, Henry's sister
- Admiral Crawford, uncle and guardian to Henry and Mary

- Mrs. Crawford, Admiral Crawford's late wife
- Miss Anderson, acquaintance of Tom Bertram
- Charles Anderson, brother of Miss Anderson
- Mrs. Holford, friend of Tom Bertram
- Sneyd, friend of Tom Bertram
- Miss Sneyd, sister of Mr. Sneyd
- Augusta Sneyd, another sister
- Mrs. Sneyd, mother of Tom Bertram's friends
- Smith, friend of Mr. Rushworth
- Humphrey Repton, well-known landscape designer in England at the time
- Captain Marshall, William Price's captain
- Mrs. Rushworth, Mr. Rushworth's mother
- Mr. Rushworth, Mrs. Rushworth's late husband
- Mr. Green, acquaintance of Mrs. Norris
- John Groom, acquaintance of Mrs. Norris
- Mrs. Jefferies, friend of Mrs. Norris
- Wilcox, Bertram's driver
- Mrs. Whitaker, Mrs. Rushworth's housekeeper
- Honourable John Yates, friend of Tom Bertram
- Right Honourable Lord Ravenshaw, friend of John Yates
- Lady Ravenshaw, wife of Lord Ravenshaw
- Sir Henry, friend of John Yates
- Christopher Jackson, carpenter
- Dick Jackson, son of Christopher Jackson
- Olivers, Bertram neighbors
- Tom Oliver, Bertram neighbor
- Charles Maddox, Bertram neighbor
- Baddely, Sir Thomas Bertram's butler
- Stephen, Bertram coachman

- Charles, Bertram coachman
- Robert, Dr. Grant's gardener
- Mrs. Brown, acquaintance of William Price
- Lucy Gregory, courted by a lieutenant in Portsmouth
- Gregorys, Portsmouth family
- Chapman, Lady Bertram's maid
- The Misses Maddox, Bertram neighbors
- Lady Prescott, Bertram neighbor
- Colonel Harrison, Bertram neighbor
- Mr. Owen, friend of Edmund
- The Misses Owen, sisters of Edmund's friend
- Sir Charles, friend of Admiral Crawford
- Mrs. Janet (Ross) Fraser, friend of Mary Crawford
- Lady (Flora Ross) Stornaway, sister of Mrs. Fraser
- Mr. Fraser, Janet Fraser's husband
- Margaret Fraser, daughter of Mr. Fraser
- Lord Stornaway, husband of Lady Stornaway
- Mr. Campbell, friend of William Price
- Susan Price, sister of Fanny
- Betsey Price, sister of Fanny
- Rebecca, the Prices' servant
- Captain Walsh, friend of Mr. Price
- Old Scholey, friend of Mr. Price
- Tom Price, brother of Fanny
- Charles Price, brother of Fanny
- Sam Price, brother of Fanny
- Sally, the Prices' maid
- Mary Price, sister of Fanny
- Mrs. Admiral Maxwell

- John Price, brother of Fanny
- Richard Price, brother of Fanny
- Aylmers, friends of the Rushworths
- Lady Lascelles, former resident of Wimpole Street
- Mr. Maddison, friend of Mr. Crawford
- Mr. Harding, friend of Mr. Bertram

- *Emma*
  - Emma Woodhouse, heroine, mistress of her father's house
  - Miss Anna Taylor, later Mrs. Weston, Emma's governess
  - Mr. Henry Woodhouse, Emma's father
  - Captain Weston, Miss Taylor's new husband
  - Isabella Woodhouse, later Knightley, Emma's sister, who married Mr. Knightley's brother
  - James, Woodhouse coachman
  - Hannah, James's daughter, housemaid at Randalls, the Weston home
  - Mr. George Knightley, longtime Woodhouse family neighbor and friend
  - Farmer Mitchell, neighbor of the Woodhouses
  - Philip Elton, vicar of Highbury
  - Miss Churchill, Mr. Weston's first wife, mother of Frank
  - Mr. Churchill, uncle and guardian of Frank
  - Mrs. Churchill, aunt and guardian of Frank
  - Frank Churchill, son of Mr. Weston
  - Mrs. Perry, neighbor of Mrs. and Miss Bates, wife of Mr. Perry
  - Mrs. Bates, widow of the former vicar of Highbury
  - Miss Hetty Bates, daughter of Mrs. Bates, with whom she lives, aunt of Jane Fairfax
  - Mr. Perry, apothecary
  - The little Perrys
  - Mrs. Goddard, boarding-school mistress

- Harriet Smith, orphan boarding at Mrs. Goddard's school, friend of Emma
- Serle, Mr. Woodhouse's cook
- Martins, friends of Harriet
- Mrs. Martin, mother of Robert Martin
- Robert Martin, suitor of Harriet Smith
- Miss Nash, teacher
- Miss Prince, teacher
- Miss Richardson, teacher
- Elizabeth Martin, sister of Robert Martin
- Miss Martin, sister of Robert Martin
- John Knightley, brother of Mr. Knightley
- Abbotts, friends of Harriet
- Mr. Cole, friend of Mr. Elton
- George Knightley, son of John and Isabella Knightley
- Henry Knightley, son
- John Knightley, son
- Bella Knightley, daughter
- Emma Knightley, daughter
- Jane Fairfax, niece of Miss Bates
- Colonel and Mrs. Campbell, guardians of Jane Fairfax
- Mr. Wingfield, Isabella Knightley's apothecary
- Mr. Graham, friend of John Knightley
- Braithwaites, friends of Frank Churchill
- William Coxe, lawyer
- Mrs. Cole, Mr. Cole's wife
- Mrs. Dixon, daughter of the Campbells
- Mr. Dixon, husband of Mrs. Dixon
- Lieutenant Fairfax, late father of Jane Fairfax

- Jane Bates, late mother of Jane Fairfax
- Augusta Hawkins, later Mrs. Elton, Mr. Elton's wife
- Mr. Green, friend of the Eltons
- Mrs. Brown, friend of the Eltons
- Anne Cox, member of a Highbury family, friend of Harriet
- The Misses Cox
- A second young Cox
- Mrs. Ford, proprietor of Highbury shop
- John Saunders, optometrist
- Patty, Miss Bates's maid
- Mrs. Wallis, friend of the Bateses
- William Larkins, manager of Donwell Abbey

- Mrs. Hodges, Mr. Knightley's servant
- Broadwood, piano salesman
- Miss and Mrs. Gilbert, Highbury family
- Mrs. Stokes, Crown proprietor
- Mr. Suckling, Mrs. Elton's brother-in-law
- Mrs. Selina Suckling, Mrs. Elton's sister
- Mrs. Partridge, friend of Mrs. Elton
- Clara Partridge, later Mrs. Jeffereys, friend of Mrs Elton
- Milmans, friends of Mrs. Elton
- Mrs. Bird, friend of Mrs. Elton
- Mrs. James Cooper, friend of Mrs. Elton
- Wright, the Eltons' housekeeper
- Tom, Weston's servant
- Mr. and Mrs. Bragge, cousins of Mr. Suckling
- Tupmans, Maple Grove residents
- Dr. Hughes, Highbury resident

- Mrs. Hughes, Highbury resident
- Mrs. Otway, Highbury resident
- George Otway, Highbury resident
- Miss Otway, Highbury resident
- Miss Caroline Otway, Highbury resident
- Mr. Arthur Otway, Highbury resident
- Miss Bickerton, boarder at Mrs. Goddard's school
- Mrs. Smallridge, friend of the Sucklings
- John Abdy, Crown manager
- Harry, servant at Donwell Abbey
- Anna Weston, Weston's daughter

Northanger Abbey

- Catherine Morland, heroine, eldest daughter of a clergyman
- Reverend Richard Morland, father of Catherine
- Mrs. Morland, Catherine's mother
- Sally (Sarah) Morland, Catherine's sister
- Mr. Allen, chief property owner of Fullerton, where the Morlands live
- Mrs. Allen, Mr. Allen's wife and Catherine's host in Bath
- Dr. Skinner and family, friends of the Allens
- Parrys, friends of the Allens
- George Parry, Parry son
- Mr. King, well-known master of ceremonies, Bath's assembly hall
- Henry Tilney, clergyman and son of General Tilney
- Mrs. Thorpe, friend of Mrs. Allen, mother of Catherine's friend Isabella Thorpe
- John Thorpe, son of Mrs. Thorpe, friend of Catherine's brother James
- Edward Thorpe, brother of John
- William Thorpe, another brother
- Isabella Thorpe, sister of John and friend of Catherine

- James Morland, Catherine's brother
- Miss Andrews, friend of Isabella
- Captain Hunt, dance partner of Isabella
- Freeman, friend of John Thorpe
- Jackson, friend of John Thorpe
- Mrs. Hughes, friend of the Tilneys
- Eleanor Tilney, Henry's sister
- Miss Drummond, the late Mrs. Tilney's maiden name
- Miss Smith, an acquaintance of Mrs. Hughes
- Sam Fletcher, friend of John Thorpe with a horse to sell
- General Tilney, Henry's father and master of Northanger Abbey
- Mitchells, friends of Isabella
- William, servant of General Tilney
- Captain Frederick Tilney, brother of Henry
- Anne Thorpe, Isabella's sister
- Maria Thorpe, Isabella's sister
- Emily, friend of Anne Thorpe
- Sophia, friend of Anne Thorpe
- Charles Hodges, potential dance partner for Isabella
- Marquis of Longtown, friend of General Tilney
- General Courteney, friend of General Tilney
- the Lady Frasers, friends of the Tilneys
- Robinson, worked for the Tilneys
- Charlotte Davis, companion of Frederick Tilney
- Anne Mitchell, acquaintance of Isabella
- Alice, Miss Tilney's maid
- George Morland, brother of Catherine
- Harriet Morland, sister of Catherine
- Richard Morland, brother of Catherine

✦ *Persuasion*

- Sir Walter Elliot, master of Kellynch Hall
- Elizabeth (Stevenson) Elliot, Sir Walter's late wife
- James Stevenson, father of Elizabeth Elliot
- Elizabeth Elliot, eldest daughter of Sir Walter
- Anne Elliot, heroine, second daughter
- Mary (Elliot) Musgrove, youngest daughter
- Charles Musgrove, husband of Mary
- Charles Musgrove, Esq., father of Charles Musgrove
- William Walter Elliot, Esq., distant cousin of Sir Walter, and Kellynch heir
- Lady Russell, widow, Elliot family friend
- John Shepherd, Sir Walter's business agent
- Sir Henry Russell, Mrs. Russell's late husband
- Penelope Clay, widow, daughter of John Shepherd and friend and confidante of Sir Walter and Elizabeth Elliot
- Lord St. Ives, acquaintance of Sir Walter
- Admiral Baldwin, acquaintance of Sir Walter
- Sir Basil Morley, acquaintance of Sir Walter
- Admiral Croft, would-be renter of Sir Walter's home
- Sophia (Sophy) Croft, Admiral Croft's wife, sister of Captain Wentworth
- Governor Trent, former resident of Monkford
- Captain Frederick Wentworth, Mrs. Croft's brother
- Little Charles Musgrove, Charles and Mary's son
- Walter Musgrove, another son
- Mackenzie, the Elliots' gardener
- Pooles, friends of the Musgroves
- Henrietta Musgrove, Charles Musgrove's sister

- Louisa Musgrove, Charles's sister
- Jemima, Musgrove housemaid
- Edward Wentworth, Captain Wentworth's brother
- Richard (Dick) Musgrove, older brother of Charles, crewman on Captain Wentworth's ship
- Mr. Robinson, apothecary
- Captain Harville, friend of Charles Musgrove
- Lady Mary Grierson, friend of the Crofts
- Mrs. Harville, Captain Harville's wife
- The Misses Hayter, Musgrove cousins
- Charles Hayter, Musgrove cousin
- Spicers, friends of the Hayters
- Dr. Shirley, rector of Uppercross
- Captain Benwick, friend of Captain Harville
- Fanny Harville, Captain Harville's sister and Captain Benwick's late betrothed
- Mrs. Shirley, wife of Dr. Shirley
- Sarah, Musgrove nursery maid
- Colonel Wallis, friend of Sir Walter
- Mrs. Wallis, wife of Colonel Wallis
- Dowager Viscountess Dalrymple, cousin of the Elliots
- Honourable Miss Carteret, daughter of Lady Dalrymple
- Miss Hamilton, later Mrs. Smith, schoolfellow of Anne
- Mrs. Speed, resident of Mrs. Smith's building
- Nurse Rooke, Mrs. Smith's nurse
- Captain Brigden, friend of Admiral Croft
- Admiral Brand, friend of Admiral Croft
- Sir Archibald Drew, friend of Admiral Croft
- Miss Atkinson, friend of William Elliot

- Lady Alicia, friend of Lady Russell
- Mrs. Frankland, friend of Lady Russell
- The Misses Larolle, concertgoers
- Durands, concertgoers
- Ibbotsons, friends of Lady Dalrymple
- Lady Mary Maclean, friend of Lady Dalrymple
- Mary, Mrs. Smith's maid
- Charles Smith, Mrs. Smith's late husband

LOCATIONS IN HER NOVELS

Real and *imaginary*, in order of first mention

- *Sense and Sensibility*
  - *Norland Park,* Sussex
  - *Stanhill,* home of Dashwood parents
  - *Barton Park*, Devonshire, home of Sir John Middleton
  - *Barton Cottage*, Devonshire, home of the Dashwoods
  - *Allenham Court*, Somersetshire, home of Willoughby's patron, Mrs. Smith
  - *High-church Down*, near Barton
  - *Whitwell*, Devonshire, twelve miles from Barton
  - Avignon, France, location of Colonel Brandon's sister
  - *Newton*, Devonshire, home of the Misses Carey
  - Honiton, Devonshire, stop on the way to London
  - *Delaford*, Dorsetshire, home of Colonel Brandon
  - Oxford, where Robert Ferrars went to school
  - *Cleveland*, Somersetshire, Palmer home

- Weymouth, Dorsetshire, home of Mrs. Palmer's uncle
- *Combe Magna*, Somersetshire, Willoughby estate
- Exeter, Devonshire, home of the Steeles
- *Longstaple*, Devonshire, home of Mr. Pratt, where Edward was schooled

- Plymouth, Devonshire, home of Edward's friends
- London
    - Hanover Square, Palmer London residence
    - Bond Street, where Willoughby was staying
    - Portman Square, near where Mrs. Jennings stayed
    - Berkeley Street, where Mrs. Jennings and the Dashwood sisters stayed
    - Bartlett's Buildings, Holburn, where the Steele's cousins were staying
    - Conduit Street, location of Middleton's London home
    - Sackville Street, location of Gray's shop
    - Harley Street, three-month home of John and Fanny Dashwood
    - Saint James Street, Colonel Brandon's lodgings
    - Park Street, Mrs. Ferrars's home
    - Pall Mall, location of Edward's lodgings
    - Kensington Gardens, where Elinor runs into Anne Steele
    - Drury Lane Theatre, where Willoughby encounters Sir John Middleton
- Scotland, where Colonel Brandon almost eloped with Fanny
- Bath, location of Eliza Williams's young friends
- *East Kingham Farm*, property adjoining Norland
- Dawlish, Devonshire, near Barton

- Dartford, Kent, Elliot home
- Norfolk, where Edward could live if he married Miss Morton
- Bristol, near *Cleveland*
- Marlborough, Wiltshire, stop on the way from London
- *Barton Cross*, site of Sir John's new plantations
- *Abbeyland*, near Colonel Brandon's home
- *Priory*, old ruins near Barton

Pride and Prejudice

- *Netherfield*, Hertfordshire, Bingley home
- *Longbourn*, Hertfordshire, Bennet home
- *Meryton*, Hertfordshire, where the militia is stationed
- *Lucas Lodge*, Hertfordshire, Lucas family home
- London
- Saint James Court, royal court of Great Britain
- Cheapside, London, where the Gardiners live
- *Hunsford*, Kent, where Mr. Collins lives
- Westerham, Kent, near Hunsford
- *Rosings*, Kent, Catherine de Bourgh's estate
- Grosvenor Street, London, home of the Hursts
- Gracechurch Street, Cheapside, Gardiner home
- The Lakes, northwest England
- Cambridge, Cambridgeshire, where Wickham attended school
- Ramsgate, Kent, where Georgiana rendezvoused with Wickham
- Bromley, borough of London
- Brighton, Sussex, militia encampment
- Liverpool, Merseyside, home of Miss King's uncle
- Matlock, Derbyshire, on Gardiners' tour with Elizabeth
- Chatsworth, Derbyshire, on Gardiners' tour with Elizabeth
- Dovedale, Derbyshire, on Gardiners' tour with Elizabeth

- · The Peak, Derbyshire, on Gardiners' tour with Elizabeth
- · Oxford, Oxfordshire, on Gardiners' tour with Elizabeth
- · Blenheim, Oxfordshire, on Gardiners' tour with Elizabeth
- · Warwick, Warwickshire, on Gardiners' tour with Elizabeth
- · Kenilworth, Warwickshire, on Gardiners' tour with Elizabeth
- · Birmingham, Warwickshire, on Gardiners' tour with Elizabeth
- · *Lambton*, Derbyshire, Mrs. Gardiner's former home and where the Gardiners and Elizabeth stayed
- · *Pemberley*, Derbyshire, Darcy's estate
- · Bakewell, Derbyshire, near Pemberley
- · Gretna Green, Scotland, Lydia and Wickham's destination
- · Clapham, Surrey, on a route to Scotland
- · Epsom, Surrey, on a route to Scotland
- · Barnet, Middlesex, on a route to Scotland
- · Hatfield, Hertfordshire, on a route to Scotland
- · Eastbourne, Sussex, near Brighton, where soldiers congregate
- · *Haye-Park*, Hertfordshire, potential home for Lydia and Wickham
- · *Stoke*, Hertfordshire, potential home for Lydia and Wickham
- · *Ashworth*, Hertfordshire, potential home for Lydia and Wickham
- · *Purvis Lodge*, Hertfordshire, potential home for Lydia and Wickham
- · Newcastle, Northumberland, home of newlyweds Lydia and Wickham
- · Saint Clement's, London, where Lydia and Wickham married
- · *Kympton*, Derbyshire, where Wickham had hoped to live once
- · Scarborough, North Yorkshire, travel destination of Georgiana's friends
- · *Oakham Mount*, Hertfordshire, near the Bennet home

- *Mansfield Park*
  - · Huntingdon, Huntingdonshire, original home of Lady Bertram
  - · *Mansfield Park*, Northampton, Bertram estate
  - · West Indies, Sir Thomas Bertram owned property there

- Woolwich, London
- Portsmouth, Hampshire, home of the Prices
- Isle of Wight
- Eton, Berkshire, Edmund's school
- Oxford, Oxfordshire, Edmund's university
- Antigua, location of a Bertram estate
- Norfolk, location of Henry Crawford's estate
- Hill Street, London, home of Admiral Crawford
- Baker Street, London, home of the Andersons
- Ramsgate, Kent, Tom Bertram visited there
- Albion Place, London, Home of the Sneyds
- *Sotherton Court*, Northamptonshire, Mr. Rushworth's home
- *Compton*, Mr. Smith's estate
- Twickenham, London, where Admiral Crawford lives
- Bath, Somersetshire, a place Henry Crawford visits
- *Everingham*, Norfolk, Henry Crawford's estate
- Westminster, London, where Henry Crawford went to school
- Cambridge, Cambridgeshire, Henry Crawford's university
- Weymouth, Dorsetshire, racetrack
- *Ecclesford*, Cornwall, home of Lord Ravenshaw
- *Stoke*, Northamptonshire, near Mansfield Park
- Tintern Abbey, subject of a picture
- Cumberland, subject of a picture
- Liverpool, where Sir Thomas Bertram's ship landed
- *Easton*, Northamptonshire, near Mansfield Park
- *Sandcroft Hill*, near Mansfield Park
- York, Yorkshire, a place in Henry Crawford's travels
- Banbury, Oxfordshire, en route to Bath for Henry Crawford
- Tunbridge, Kent, not the country, according to Edmund

- Cheltenham, Gloucestershire, also not the country
- Brighton, Sussex, honeymoon destination of Maria and Mr. Rushworth
- Saint Paul's Cathedral, London
- English Channel, Spithead, Mediterranean Sea, Gibraltar, travels of William Price's ship
- *Thornton Lacey*, Northamptonshire, Edmund's upcoming parsonage
- Beachey Head, Sussex, near Brighton
- Peterborough, Huntingdonshire, nearby location of Edmund's friend
- *Stanwix Lodge*, near Mansfield Park
- *Lessingby*, Huntingdonshire, Edmund visits there
- Newbury, Berkshire, Fanny travels here en route to Portsmouth
- High Street, Portsmouth, near the Price's house
- Turner's, naval supply store in Portsmouth
- Texel, island off the Dutch coast
- Wimpole Street, London, where Maria Rushworth stayed
- Saint George's, Hanover Square, London, church
- Newmarket, Suffolk, place where Tom Bertram caroused with friends
- Bedford Square, London, home of Julia's cousins
- Richmond, town west of London, where Henry Crawford stayed
- Scotland, Julia and Mr. Yates's elopement destination

- *Emma*
  - London, where Emma's sister lived
  - *Hartfield*, home of the Woodhouses
  - *Highbury*, Surrey, "large and populous village" and location of Hartfield
  - *Randalls*, home of the Westons
  - Brunswick Square, London, home of John and Isabella Knightley
  - *Broadway-lane*, near Randalls
  - *Enscombe*, Yorkshire, home of Mr. Weston's first wife's family

- *Donwell Abbey*, Surrey, Mr. Knightley's estate
- *Abbey-Mill Farm*, where the Martins live
- Kingston, Surrey, Mr. Martin travels there
- *Donwell Road*, neighborhood road
- Bond Street, London, where Emma's picture of Harriet was framed
- *Clayton Park*, Mr. Perry visited there
- *Vicarage Lane*, where Mr. Elton's house was situated
- Cobham, Surrey, near Highbury
- Weymouth, Dorsetshire, Frank traveled there
- South End, Essex, where John and Isabella Knightley vacationed
- Cromer, Norfolk, seaside vacation spot
- *Langham*, near Donwell
- Bath, Somersetshire, a place Mrs. Elton called home
- Dublin, Ireland, where the Dixons live
- *Baly-Craig*, Ireland, Dixon residence
- Holyhead, Wales, port on the way to Ireland
- Bristol, Mrs. Elton's hometown
- White-Hart, Bath, destination of Mr. Elton's trunk
- Oxford, Frank stops here en route to Highbury
- *Crown*, business in Highbury
- *Ford's*, shop in Highbury
- *Maple Grove*, Gloucestershire, home of the Sucklings
- King's-Weston, Bristol, grand estate
- Clifton, Bristol, a place Mrs. Churchill might want to recuperate
- *West Hall*, Tupman residence
- Birmingham, Warwickshire, original home of Tupmans
- Richmond, town west of London, Frank's aunt stayed there
- Manchester Street, Richmond, location of Frank's aunt
- Box Hill, Surrey, picnic site

- Saint Mark's Place, Venice, picture subject
- Swisserland, picture subject
- Mickleham, Surrey, neighboring town
- Dorking, Surrey, neighboring town
- Windsor, Berkshire, location of Frank's friend

♦ *Northanger Abbey*

- *Fullerton*, Wiltshire, home of the Morlands
- Bath, Somersetshire, where Catherine Morland's adventures begin
  - Pulteney Street, Allen's lodgings
  - Upper Rooms, dance hall
  - Pump Room, popular gathering spot
  - Lower Rooms, dance hall
- Salisbury, Wiltshire, town near the Morlands
- Gloucestershire, where the Tilneys reside
- Oxford, Oxfordshire, where John Thorpe was a student
- Merchant-Taylors' School, London, where Edward Thorpe was a student
- Tunbridge, Kent, Isabella Thorpe attended balls there
- London, Isabella visited there
- Bath Crescent, row of houses with a promenade
- Milsom Street, Bath, shopping district
- Edgar's Buildings, Bath, where the Thorpes stayed
- Union Passage, Bath, route for Isabella
- Cheap Street, Bath, route for Isabella
- London Road, Bath, busy thoroughfare
- Oxford Road, Bath, busy thoroughfare
- Tetbury, Gloucester, destination of outing for Thorpes and Morlands
- Walcot Church, Bath, landmark
- Magdalen Bridge, Oxford, John Thorpe met a friend there

- Christchurch, home of John Thorpe's friend Freeman
- Oriel, Oxford college, where John Thorpe's friend Jackson is a student
- Lansdown Hill, suburb of Bath, outing destination
- Octagon Room, Bath, dance hall
- Claverton Down, southeastern suburb of Bath
- Leicestershire, John Thorpe considers getting a house there
- Bristol, outing destination
- Clifton, Bristol, outing destination
- Kingsweston, Bristol, grand estate, outing destination
- Blaize Castle, Bristol, outing destination
- Bath

Broad Street	Argyle Street
Lansdown Road	The Bedford
Laura Place	Bond Street
Argyle Buildings	York Hotel

- Keynsham, Somersetshire, as far as the Thorpe party traveled
- Beechen Cliff, hill on the edge of Bath
- Saint George's Field, the Bank, the Tower of London, Catherine's imagined settings of Frederick Tilney's military conquests
- Northampton, Northamptonshire, where Frederick is stationed
- Richmond, town west of London, where Isabella wants to settle
- Putney, Surrey, the Thorpes' hometown
- Devizes, Wiltshire, John Thorpe destination
- *Northanger Abbey*, Gloucestershire, thirty miles outside of Bath, home of the Tilneys
- Petty France, on the way to Northanger Abbey from Bath
- *Woodston*, Gloucestershire, Henry Tilney's home
- Chapel of Saint Anthony, church near Northanger Abbey

- *Brockham*, Gloucestershire, where the surveyor lives
- Bath Street, Bath, where shops are located
- Hereford, Herefordshire, Tilneys plan to travel there

◆ *Persuasion*

- *Kellynch Hall*, Somersetshire, Sir Walter Elliot's home
- *South Park*, Gloucester, the late Mrs. Elliot's home
- *Uppercross*, Somerset, home of Charles Musgrove, Esq.
- Cheshire, where Elliot ancestors first settled
- London, Sir Walter and Elizabeth's travel destination
- Tattersall's, London, horse auctioneers
- House of Commons, London
- Bath, where the Elliots moved
- *Kellynch Lodge*, Somersetshire, Lady Russell's home
- Taunton, Somersetshire, location of quarter sessions
- *Monkford*, Somersetshire, where Edward Wentworth was once a curate
- Santo Domingo, Captain Wenworth took action there
- Thames River, London
- *Uppercross Cottage*, Somersetshire, home of the Charles and Mary Musgrove family
- *Great House, Uppercross*, home of Charles's parents and sisters
- Exeter, Devonshire, where Henrietta and Louisa were schooled
- Queen Square, Bath, Elliots advised not to live there
- Clifton, Bristol, travel stop
- Plymouth, Devonshire, Wentworth sailed Harvilles there
- The Sound, bay at Plymouth
- Gibraltar, where Richard Musgrove fell ill
- Western Islands, Azores, Wentworth's friend cruised there
- Mediterranean, Wentworth sailed there

- Portsmouth, Hampshire, port
- Atlantic Ocean, East Indies, Cork, Lisbon, Gibraltar, Streights, Bermuda, Bahamas, places the Crofts have traveled
- Deal, Kent, Mrs. Croft stayed there while her husband was away
- North Seas, where Admiral Croft sailed
- Shropshire, home of Wentworth's brother
- *Winthrop*, Somersetshire, would-be home of Charles Hayter
- North Yarmouth, Isle of Wight, where the Crofts first lived
- Lyme Regis, Devonshire, home of the Harvilles
- The Cobb, Lyme, where Louisa fell
- Charmouth, Dorsetshire, near Lyme
- Up Lyme, Dorsetshire, scenic area near Lyme
- Pinny, Dorsetshire, scenic area near Lyme
- Isle of Wight, Lyme compares in beauty
- Sidmouth, Devonshire, William Elliot traveled there
- Crewkherne, Somersetshire, chaise sent to Charles from there
- Cape of Good Hope, Captain Harville sailed there
- Camden Place, Bath, the Elliots' new home
- Old Bridge, Bath, en route to Camden Place
- Rivers Street, Bath, Lady Russell's lodgings
- Marlborough Buildings, Bath, Colonel Wallis's home
- Lansdown Crescent, Bath, where Mr. Elliot dined
- Laura Place, Bath, Lady Dalrymple's house for three months
- Westgate Buildings, Bath, Mrs. Smith's lodgings
- Gay Street, Bath, Croft's lodgings
- Milsom Street, Bath
- Belmont, Bath, quiet street
- Minehead, Somersetshire, Croft's visited there
- Union Street, Bath, errand destination for Mr. Elliot

- Pulteney Street, Bath, Anne spots Captain Wentworth
- Octagon Room, Bath, Lady Dalrymple's concert venue
- Tunbridge Wells, Kent, home of Charles Smith
- *Thornberry Park*, near Bath
- Pump Room, Bath
- Bath Street, Bath
- Pump Yard, Bath, open area just north of the Pump Room
- Market Place, Bath street

LITERARY REFERENCES IN ORDER OF MENTION

- *Sense and Sensibility*
  - William Cowper
  - Sir Walter Scott
  - Alexander Pope
  - *Hamlet*, William Shakespeare
  - James Thomson
  - *Columella; or, The Distressed Anchoret*, Richard Graves
- *Pride and Prejudice*
  - *Sermons to Young Women*, James Fordyce
- *Mansfield Park*
  - *Paradise Lost*, John Milton
  - *The Task*, William Cowper
  - *The Lay of the Last Minstrel*, Sir Walter Scott
  - *Sermons*, Hugh Blair
  - *Quarterly Review*

- *Lovers' Vows*, from the German of Kotzebue, translated by Mrs. Inchbald
- *My Grandmother*, Prince Hoare
- *Merchant of Venice*, William Shakespeare
- *Richard III*, William Shakespeare
- *Julius Caesar*, William Shakespeare
- *Hamlet*, William Shakespeare
- *Macbeth*, William Shakespeare
- *Othello*, William Shakespeare
- *Douglas: A Tragedy*, John Home
- *The Gamester: A Tragedy*, Edward Moore
- *The Rivals*, Richard Brinsley Sheridan
- *The School for Scandal*, Richard Brinsley Sheridan
- *Wheel of Fortune: A Comedy*, Richard Cumberland
- *Heir at Law*, George Colman
- *Journal of the Embassy to China*, Lord Macartney
- *Tales*, George Crabbe
- *The Idler*, a periodical published by Samuel Johnson
- *Address to Tobacco*, Isaac Hawkins Browne
- *Henry VIII*, William Shakespeare
- The Book of Common Prayer
- *The History of Rasselas, Prince of Abyssinia*, Dr. Johnson
- *History of England*, Oliver Goldsmith
- *Tirocinium*, William Cowper
- *A Sentimental Journey*, Laurence Sterne
- "The Je Ne Scai Quoi: A Song," William Whitehead

* *Emma*
  - *Agricultural Reports*
  - *Elegant Extracts*

- *Vicar of Wakefield*, Oliver Goldsmith
- *The Romance of the Forest*, Ann Radcliffe
- *Children of the Abbey*, Regina Maria Roche
- *A Midsummer Night's Dream*, William Shakespeare
- "Kitty, a fair but frozen maid," *The Poetical Works of David Garrick*
- Psalm 16
- "Elegy," Thomas Gray
- "L'Allegro," John Milton
- "The Winter Evening," William Cowper
- *Romeo and Juliet*, William Shakespeare
- *Fables: The Hare and Many Friends*, John Gay
- *Adelaide and Theodore*, Madame de Genlis
- Book of Common Prayer
- Music

    Johann Baptist Cramer

    "Robin Adair"
- Charades

My first doth affliction denote
Which my second is destin'd to fee.
And my whole is the best antidote
That affliction to soften and heal.

My first displays the wealth and pomp of kings,
Lords of the earth! their luxury and ease.

Another view of man, my second brings,
Behold him there, the monarch of the seas!
But ah! united, what reverse we have!
Man's boasted power and freedom, all are flown;
Lord of the earth and sea, he bends a slave,
And woman, lovely woman, reigns alone.
Thy ready wit the word will soon supply,
May its approval beam in that soft eye!

- *Northanger Abbey*
  - "The Beggar's Petition," Thomas Moss
  - *Fables: The Hare and Many Friends*, John Gay
  - "Elegy to the Memory of an Unfortunate Lady," Alexander Pope
  - "Elegy Written in a Country Churchyard," Thomas Gray
  - *The Seasons*, James Thomson
  - *Othello*, William Shakespeare
  - *Measure for Measure*, William Shakespeare
  - *Twelfth Night*, William Shakespeare
  - *The Rambler,* Samuel Richardson
  - *History of England*
  - John Milton
  - Matthew Prior
  - *The Spectator*
  - Laurence Sterne
  - *Cecelia; or, Memoirs of an Heiress*, Frances Burney
  - *Camilla; or, A Picture of Youth*, Frances Burney
  - *Belinda*, Maria Edgeworth
  - *The Mysteries of Udolpho*, Ann Radcliffe

- *The Italian; or, The Confessional of the Black Penitents*, Ann Radcliffe
- *Castle of Wolfenbach*, Eliza Parsons
- *Clermont*, Regina Maria Roche
- *Mysterious Warnings*, Eliza Parsons
- *Necromancer of the Black Forest*, Peter Teuthold
- *Midnight Bell*, Francis Lathom
- *Orphan of the Rhine*, Eleanor Sleath
- *Horrid Mysteries*, Peter Will
- *Sir Charles Grandison*, Samuel Richardson
- *Tom Jones*, Henry Fielding
- *The Monk*, Mathew Gregory Lewis
- *Dictionary*, Samuel Johnson
- Hugh Blair
- *The History of England*, David Hume
- William Robertson
- *The Mirror*, Henry Mackenzie

- *Persuasion*
  - *Baronetage*
  - *Cheshire Visitation Pedigrees*, Sir William Dugdale
  - *Marmion*, Sir Walter Scott
  - *The Lady of the Lake*, Sir Walter Scott
  - *The Giaour*, Lord Byron
  - *The Bride of Abydos*, Lord Byron
  - *The Corsair*, Lord Byron
  - *Henry and Emma*, Matthew Prior
  - *An Essay on Criticism*, Alexander Pope
  - *Scheherazade*

THE HEROINES

+ *Sense and Sensibility*
  Elinor Dashwood

"She had an excellent heart;—her disposition was affectionate, and her feelings were strong; but she knew how to govern them: it was a knowledge which her mother had yet to learn, and which one of her sisters had resolved never to be taught."

+ *Pride and Prejudice*
  Elizabeth Bennet

"Elizabeth, easy and unaffected."

+ *Mansfield Park*
  Fanny Price

"Fanny Price was at this time just ten years old, and though there might not be much in her first appearance to captivate, there was, at least, nothing to disgust her relations."

+ *Emma*
  Emma

"The real evils, indeed, of Emma's situation were the power of having rather too much her own way, and a disposition to think a little too well of herself; these were the disadvantages which threatened alloy to her many enjoyments."

+ *Northanger Abbey*
  Catherine Morland

"She had a thin awkward figure, a sallow skin without colour, dark lank hair, and strong features—so much for her person; and not less unpropitious for *heroism seemed her mind. She was fond of all boy's plays, and greatly preferred cricket not merely to dolls, but to the more heroic enjoyments of infancy, nursing a dormouse, feeding a canary-bird, or watering a rose-bush."*

❀ *Persuasion*
Anne Elliot

"But Anne, with an elegance of mind and sweetness of character, which must have placed her high with any people of real understanding, was nobody with either father or sister; her word had no weight, her convenience was always to give way—she was only Anne."

THE HEROES

❀ *Sense and Sensibility*
Edward Ferrars, would-be clergyman

"He was not handsome, and his manners required intimacy to make them pleasing. He was too diffident to do justice to himself; but when his natural shyness was overcome, his behaviour gave every indication of an open affectionate heart. His understanding was good, and his education had given it solid improvement."

❀ *Pride and Prejudice*
Fitzwilliam Darcy, landowner

"But his friend Mr. Darcy soon drew the attention of the room by his fine, tall person, handsome features, noble mien, and the report which was in general circulation within five minutes after his entrance, of his having ten thousand a year."

◆ *Mansfield Park*
   Edmund Bertram, would-be clergyman

"*Strong good sense and uprightness of mind.*"

◆ *Emma*
   Mr. Knightley, landowner

"*A sensible man about seven or eight-and-thirty, was not only a very old and intimate friend of the family, but particularly connected with it, as the elder brother of Isabella's husband.*"

◆ *Northanger Abbey*
   Henry Tilney, would-be clergyman

"*His manner might sometimes surprise, but his meaning must always be just.*"

◆ *Persuasion*
   Captain Wentworth, retired naval captain

"*He had been lucky in his profession; but spending freely, what had come freely, had realized nothing. But he was confident that he should soon be rich: full of life and ardour, he knew that he should soon have a ship, and soon be on a station that would lead to everything he wanted.*"

◆ *Lady Susan*
   Sir Reginald De Courcy, heir

"*You must be sensible that as an only son, and the representative of an ancient family, your conduct in life is most interesting to your connections; and in the very important concern of marriage especially, there is everything at stake—your own happiness, that of your parents, and the credit of your name.*"

THE CADS

♦ *Sense and Sensibility*
John Willoughby, potential heir

"His manly beauty and more than common gracefulness were instantly the theme of general admiration, and the laugh which his gallantry raised against Marianne, received particular spirit from his exterior attractions."

♦ *Pride and Prejudice*
George Wickham, lieutenant in the militia

"Mr. Wickham was the happy man towards whom almost every female eye was turned."

♦ *Mansfield Park*
Henry Crawford, estate owner and heir

"Henry Crawford, ruined by early independence and bad domestic example, indulged in the freaks of a cold-blooded vanity a little too long."

♦ *Emma*
Frank Churchill, heir

"Mr. Frank Churchill was one of the boasts of Highbury, and a lively curiosity to see him prevailed, though the compliment was so little returned that he had never been there in his life."

♦ *Northanger Abbey*
Captain Tilney, military officer

"His taste and manners were beyond a doubt decidedly inferior."

* *Persuasion*
  William Walter Elliot, potential heir

"Instead of pushing his fortune in the line marked out for the heir of the house of Elliot, he had purchased independence by uniting himself to a rich woman of inferior birth."

THE VIXENS

* *Lady Susan*
  Lady Susan, widow

"Her neglect of her husband, her encouragement of other men, her extravagance and dissipation, were so gross and notorious that no one could be ignorant of them at the time, nor can now have forgotten them."

* *Sense and Sensibility*
  Lucy Steele

"Could he ever be tolerably happy with Lucy Steele; could he, were his affection for herself out of the question, with his integrity, his delicacy, and well-informed mind, be satisfied with a wife like her—illiterate, artful, and selfish?"

* *Mansfield Park*
  Mary Crawford

"Matrimony was her object, provided she could marry well."

* *Northanger Abbey*
  Isabella Thorpe

"Isabella—no wonder now I have not heard from her—Isabella has deserted my brother, and is to marry yours! Could you have believed there had been such inconstancy and fickleness, and everything that is bad in the world?"

+ *Persuasion*
  Mrs. Clay

"*Mrs Clay had freckles, and a projecting tooth, and a clumsy wrist, which he was continually making severe remarks upon, in her absence; but she was young, and certainly altogether well-looking, and possessed, in an acute mind and assiduous pleasing manners, infinitely more dangerous attractions than any merely personal might have been.*"

VICARS WHO ARE NOT HEROES

+ *Pride and Prejudice*
  Mr. Collins

"*The subjection in which his father had brought him up had given him originally great humility of manner; but it was now a good deal counteracted by the self-conceit of a weak head, living in retirement, and the consequential feelings of early and unexpected prosperity.*"

+ *Emma*
  Mr. Elton

"*I do own myself to have been completely mistaken in Mr. Elton. There is a littleness about him which you discovered, and which I did not.*"

INJURIES THAT LED TO ROMANCE

+ *Sense and Sensibility*

"*[Marianne] had raised herself from the ground, but her foot had been twisted in the fall, and she was scarcely able to stand. The gentleman offered his services, and perceiving that her modesty declined what her situation rendered necessary, took her up in his arms without farther delay, and carried her down the hill."*

❖ *Pride and Prejudice*

"Well, my dear," said Mr. Bennet, when Elizabeth had read the note aloud, "if your daughter [Jane] should have a dangerous fit of illness—if she should die, it would be a comfort to know that it was all in pursuit of Mr. Bingley, and under your orders."

❖ *Persuasion*

"[Louisa] was safely down, and instantly, to show her enjoyment, ran up the steps to be jumped down again. He advised her against it, thought the jar too great; but no, he reasoned and talked in vain, she smiled and said, 'I am determined I will:' he put out his hands; she was too precipitate by half a second, she fell on the pavement on the Lower Cobb, and was taken up lifeless!"

HUMILIATION AT BALLS

❖ *Sense and Sensibility*

"They had not remained in this manner long, before Elinor perceived Willoughby, standing within a few yards of them, in earnest conversation with a very fashionable looking young woman. She soon caught his eye, and he immediately bowed, but without attempting to speak to her, or to approach Marianne, though he could not but see her; and then continued his discourse with the same lady. Elinor turned involuntarily to Marianne, to see whether it could be unobserved by her. At that moment she first perceived him, and her

whole countenance glowing with sudden delight, she would have moved towards him instantly, had not her sister caught hold of her."

+ *Pride and Prejudice*

"'Which do you mean?' and turning round he looked for a moment at Elizabeth, till catching her eye, he withdrew his own and coldly said: 'She is tolerable, but not handsome enough to tempt me; I am in no humour at present to give consequence to young ladies who are slighted by other men. You had better return to your partner and enjoy her smiles, for you are wasting your time with me.'"

+ *Mansfield Park*

"They had talked, and they had been silent; he [Henry] had reasoned, she [Miss Crawford] had ridiculed; and they had parted at last with mutual vexation. Fanny, not able to refrain entirely from observing them, had seen enough to be tolerably satisfied. It was barbarous to be happy when Edmund was suffering. Yet some happiness must and would arise from the very conviction that he did suffer."

+ *Emma*

"But Emma's wonder lessened soon afterwards, on seeing Mr. Elton sauntering about. He would not ask Harriet to dance if it were possible to be avoided: she was sure he would not—and she was expecting him every moment to escape into the card-room."

+ *Northanger Abbey*

"She could not help being vexed at the non-appearance of Mr. Thorpe, for she not only longed to be dancing, but was likewise aware that, as the real dignity of her situation could not be known, she was sharing with the scores of other young ladies still sitting down all the discredit of wanting a partner. To be disgraced in the eye of the world, to wear the appearance of infamy while her heart is all purity, her actions all innocence, and the misconduct of another the true source of her debasement, is one of those circumstances which peculiarly belong to the heroine's life, and her fortitude under it what particularly dignifies her character."

♦ *Persuasion*

"These were some of the thoughts which occupied Anne, while her fingers were mechanically at work, proceeding for half an hour together, equally without error, and without consciousness. Once she felt that he was looking at herself, observing her altered features, perhaps, trying to trace in them the ruins of the face which had once charmed him; and once she knew that he must have spoken of her; she was hardly aware of it, till she heard the answer; but then she was sure of his having asked his partner whether Miss Elliot never danced? The answer was, "Oh, no; never; she has quite given up dancing. She had rather play. She is never tired of playing.""

What Happened to the Characters?

"In this traditionary way we learned that Miss Steele never succeeded in catching the Doctor; that Kitty Bennet was satisfactorily married to a clergyman near Pemberley, while Mary obtained nothing higher than one other uncle Philip's clerks, and was content to be considered a star in the society of Meriton; that the 'considerable sum' given by Mrs Norris to William Price was one pound; that Mr Woodhouse survived his daughter's marriage, and kept her and Mr Knightley from settling at Donwell, about two years; and that the letters placed by Frank Churchill before Jane Fairfax, which she swept away unread, contained the word 'pardon'."

—JAMES EDWARD AUSTEN-LEIGH AND ANNA LEFROY

LITERARY JOURNAL REVIEWS OF HER BOOKS AT PUBLICATION

First Sentences of Judgment

♦ *Sense and Sensibility*

· *The Critical Review*, anonymous, February 1812

"*A genteel, well-written novel is as agreeable a lounge as a genteel comedy, from which both amusement and instruction may be derived.* Sense and Sensibility *is one amongst the few, which can claim this fair praise.*"

· *The British Critic*, anonymous, May 1812

"*We think so favourably of this performance that it is with some reluctance we decline inserting it among our principal articles, but the productions of the press are so continually multiplied, that it requires all our exertions to keep tolerable pace with them.*"

♦ *Pride and Prejudice*

· *The British Critic*, anonymous, February 1813

"*We had occasion to speak favorably of the former production of this author or authoress, specified above, and we readily do the same of the present. It is very far superior to almost all the publications of the kind which have lately come before us.*"

· *The Critical Review*, anonymous, March 1813

"*Instead of the whole interest of the tale hanging upon one or two characters, as is generally the case in novels, the fair author of the present introduces us, at once, to a whole family, every individual of which excites the interest, and very agreeably divides the attention of the reader."*

· *The New Review; or, Monthly Analysis of General Literature*,
anonymous, April 1813

"The commencement of the novel introduces us to the different members of a family party, whose characters it may not be improper to sketch, for the better comprehension of the story. Mr. Bennet is a man of considerable good sense, partially shaded by his eccentricity of manner."

❖ *Mansfield Park*
· No known reviews.

❖ *Emma*
· *Quarterly Review*, Sir Walter Scott wrote it anonymously, 1816

"The author's knowledge of the world, and the peculiar tact with which she presents characters that the reader cannot fail to recognize, reminds us something of the merits of the Flemish school of painting. The subjects are not often elegant, and certainly never grand; but they are finished up to nature, and with a precision which delights the reader."

· *The Champion*, anonymous, March 31, 1816

"The imitative arts—and novel-writing is the art of imitating in a narrative the scenes of life—are productive of two distinct gratifications;—one, arising from the intrinsic beauty of grandeur of the objects represented, and the other, from the skill of the artist, shown in representing objects of an ordinary, and at the same time so familiar a nature, as to invite an easy comparison between the prototype and the imitation, and to draw intellectual faculties into a pleasing criticism on the merits of his imitative efforts. The latter, rather than the former,

is the principal attraction which we hold out to our readers in recommending to them the volumes before us. One rare merit they possess, is an entire freedom from anything like the pretence or technicality of authorship."

· *The Augustan Review*, anonymous, May 1816

"There is a remarkable sameness in the productions of this author. The Emma and Knightley of the work before us, are exactly the Elizabeth and Davey [sic] of 'Pride and Prejudice;' the prototypes of which were the hero and heroine in 'Sense and Sensibility.'"

· *British Critic*, anonymous, July 1816

"Whoever is fond of an amusing, inoffensive and well principled novel, will be well pleased with perusal of Emma. It rarely happens that in a production of this nature we have so little to find fault with."

· *Monthly Review*, anonymous, July 1816

"If this novel can scarcely be termed a composition, because it contains but one ingredient, that one is, however, of sterling worth; being a strain of genuine humour, such as is seldom found conjointly with the complete purity of images and ideas which is here conspicuous."

· *British Lady's Magazine and Monthly Miscellany*, anonymous,
   September 1816

"With notice these two works together, because we think both evince the truth of an observation we made in our last number in the Anitiquary; namely, that two or three novels generally exhaust the inventive faculties of authors in this line....and Emma falls not only below Pride and Prejudice (probably the most pleasant novel of the last half dozen years), but also of Mansfield Park, a later production of the same author."

· *Gentleman's Magazine*, anonymous, September 1816

"If 'Emma' has not the highly-drawn characters in superior life which are so interesting in 'Pride and Prejudice;' it delineates with great accuracy the habits and manners of a middle class of gentry; and of the inhabitants of country village at one degree of rank and gentility beneath them. Every character throughout the work, from the heroine to the most subordinate, is a portrait which comes home to the heart and feelings of the Reader; who becomes familiarly acquainted with each of them, nor loses sight of a single individual till the completion of the work."

· *Literary Panorama*, anonymous, June 1817

"Emma presents the history of a young lady, who, after allowing her imagination to wander towards several gentlemen, and almost to mislead her affections, fixes them, at last, on the proper object. This, we are persuaded, is no uncommon case. The story is not ill conceived; it is not romantic but domestic."

✦ *Northanger Abbey* and *Persuasion*

· *British Critic*, anonymous, March 1818

"Northanger Abbey and Persuasion, are the productions of a pen, from which our readers have already received several admired productions; and it is with most unfeigned regret, that we are forced to add, they will be the last."

· *Edinburgh Magazine and Literary Miscellany*, May 1818

"We are happy to receive two other novels from the pen of this amiable and agreeable authoress, though our satisfaction is much alloyed, from the feeling, that they must be the last. We have always regarded her works as possessing a higher claim to public estimation than perhaps they have yet obtained."

· *The Gentleman's Magazine*, July 1818

"The two Novels now published have no connexion with each other. The

characters in both are principally taken from the middle ranks of life, and are well supported. Northanger Abbey, however, is a decidedly preferable to the second Novel, not only in the incidents, but even in its moral tendency."

> · *Quarterly Review*, anonymous (known to be written by Richard Whately), January 1821

"We already begin to fear, that we have indulged too much in extracts, and we must save some room for Persuasion, *or we could not resist giving a specimen of John Thorpe, with his horse that cannot go less than 10 miles an hour, his refusal to drive his sister 'because she has such thick ankles,' and his sober consumption of five pints of port a day; altogether the best portrait of a species, which, though almost extinct, cannot be quite classed among the Palaeotheria, the Bang-up Oxonian. . . . The latter of these novels, however,* Persuasion, *which is more strictly to be considered as a posthumous work, possesses that superiority which might be expected from the more mature age at which it was written, and is second, we think, to none of the former ones, if not superior to all."*

REVIEWS BY CELEBRITIES AND TASTEMAKERS OF THE DAY

- ❖ Playwright Sheridan on *Pride and Prejudice*: advised a dinner party companion to "buy it immediately," for it was "one of the cleverest things he ever read."
- ❖ Annabella Milbanke, the future Lady Byron: "I have finished the novel called *Pride & Prejudice*, which I think a very superior work. It depends not on any of the common resources of Novel writers, no drownings,

nor conflagrations, nor runaway horses, nor lap-dogs &
parrots, nor chambermaids & milliners, nor rencontres
and disguises. I really think it is the most *probable* fiction I
have ever read. It is not a crying book, but the interest is
very strong, especially for Mr. Darcy."

- Lady Jane Davy: "'Pride and Prejudice' I do not like very
  much. Want of interest is the fault I can least excuse in
  works of mere amusement, and however natural the
  picture of vulgar minds and manners is there given, it is
  unrelieved by the agreeable contrast of more dignified and
  refined characters occasionally captivating attention."

- Mary Russell Mitford: "I would almost cut off one of my hands,
  if it would enable me to write like your aunt with the other."

- Maria Edgeworth on *Emma*: "There is no story in it,
  except that Miss Emma found that the man whom she
  designed for Harriet's lover was an admirer of her—& he
  was affronted at being refused by Emma & Harriet wore
  the willow—and smooth, thin water gruel is according
  to Emma's father's opinion a very good thing & it is very
  difficult to make a cook understand what you mean by
  smooth thin water gruel!!!"

- Susan Ferrier, author of *Marriage*, on *Emma*: "I have been
  reading 'Emma', which is excellent; there is no story
  whatever, and the heroine is not better than other people;
  but the characters are all so true to life, and the style so
  piquant, that it does not require the adventitious aids of
  mystery and adventure."

- Mary Russell Mitford on *Emma*: "By-the-way, how delightful
  is her 'Emma!' the best, I think, of all her charming works."

HER FIRST WORK, FIRST CHAPTER

To Miss Lloyd
My dear Martha

As a small testimony of the gratitude I feel for your late generosity to me in finishing my muslin Cloak, I beg leave to offer you this little production of your sincere Freind

The Author
Frederic & Elfrida
a novel

CHAPTER THE FIRST

The Uncle of Elfrida was the Father of Frederic; in other words, they were first cousins by the Father's side.

Being both born in one day & both brought up at one school, it was not wonderfull that they should look on each other with something more than bare politeness. They loved with mutual sincerity, but were both determined not to transgress the rules of Propriety by owning their attachment, either to the object beloved, or to any one else.

They were exceedingly handsome and so much alike, that it was not every one who knew them apart. Nay, even their most intimate freinds had nothing to distinguish them by, but the shape of the face, the colour of the Eye, the length of the Nose & the difference of the complexion.

Elfrida had an intimate freind to whom, being on a visit to an Aunt, she wrote the following Letter.

To Miss Drummond
Dear Charlotte

I should be obliged to you, if you would buy me, during your stay with

Mrs Williamson, a new & fashionable Bonnet, to suit the complexion of your

E. Falknor

Charlotte, whose character was a willingness to oblige every one, when she returned into the Country, brought her Freind the wished-for Bonnet, & so ended this little adventure, much to the satisfaction of all parties.

On her return to Crankhumdunberry (of which sweet village her father was Rector), Charlotte was received with the greatest Joy by Frederic & Elfrida, who, after pressing her alternately to their Bosoms, proposed to her to take a walk in a Grove of Poplars which led from the Parsonage to a verdant Lawn enamelled with a variety of variegated flowers & watered by a purling Stream, brought from the Valley of Tempé by a passage under ground.

In this Grove they had scarcely remained above 9 hours, when they were suddenly agreably surprized by hearing a most delightfull voice warble the following stanza.

SONG

That Damon was in love with me
I once thought & beleiv'd
But now that he is not I see,
I fear I was deceiv'd.

No sooner were the lines finished than they beheld by a turning in the Grove 2 elegant young women leaning on each other's arm, who immediately on perceiving them, took a different path & disappeared from their sight.

HER LAST WORK

ST. SWITHIN'S DAY
Written three days before she died

When Winchester races first took their beginning
It is said the good people forgot their old Saint
Not applying at all for the leave of St. Swithin
And that William of Wykham's approval was faint.

The races however were fix'd and determin'd
The company met & the weather was charming
The Lords & the Ladies were sattin'd & ermin'd
And nobody saw any future alarming.

But when the old Saint was inform'd of these doings
He made but one spring from his shrine to the roof
Of the Palace which now lies so sadly in ruins
And thus he address'd them all standing aloof.

Oh, subject rebellious, Oh Venta depraved
When once we are buried you think we are dead

But behold me Immortal.—By vice you're enslaved
You have sinn'd & must suffer.—Then further he said

These races & revels & dissolute measures
With which you're debasing a neighbourly Plain
Let them stand—you shall meet with a curse in your pleasures
Set off for your course, I'll pursue with my rain,

Ye cannot but know my command o'er July,
Henceforward I'll triumph in shewing my powers,
Shift your race as you will it shall never be dry
The curse upon Venta is July in showers.

JANE AND HER CHARACTERS' LISTS

FROM HER LETTERS

◆ Steventon, December 24, 1798

Our ball was very thin, but by no means unpleasant. There were thirty-one people, and only eleven ladies out of the number, and but five single women in the room. Of the gentlemen present you may have some idea from the list of my partners—Mr. Wood, G. Lefroy, Rice, a Mr. Butcher (belonging to the Temples, a sailor and not of the 11th Light Dragoons), Mr. Temple (not the horrid one of all), Mr. Wm. Orde (cousin to the Kingsclere man), Mr. John Harwood, and Mr. Calland, who appeared as usual with his hat in his hand, and stood every now and then behind Catherine and me to be talked to and abused for not dancing.

◆ Queen Square, Bath, May 1799

There was a very long list of arrivals here in the newspaper yesterday, so that we need not immediately dread absolute solitude; and there is a public breakfast in Sydney Gardens every morning, so that we shall not be wholly starved.

◆ Southampton, February 8, 1807

The Browns are added to our list of acquaintance.

◆ Southampton, February 20, 1807

I am obliged to Fanny for the list of Mrs. Coleman's children, whose names I had not, however, quite forgot; the new one I am sure will be Caroline.

PROFITS OF MY NOVELS, OVER & ABOVE THE £600 IN THE NAVY FIVES.*

	£
Residue for the 1st Edit: of Mansfield Park, ⎫ Remaining in Henrietta St—March, 1816 ⎭	13.7——
Recd from Egerton, one 2nd Edit: of Sense & S— ⎫ March 1816—— ⎭	12.15——
Feb: 21. ⎫ 1817 ⎭ First Profits of Emma————	38.18——
March 7. ⎫ 1817 ⎭ From Egerton—2nd Edit: S & S.——	19.13——

FROM HER NOVELS

⬦ *Pride and Prejudice*

"'All young ladies accomplished! My dear Charles, what do you mean?'

'Yes, all of them, I think. They all paint tables, cover screens, and net purses. I scarcely know any one who cannot do all this, and I am sure I never heard a young lady spoken of for the first time, without being informed that she was very accomplished.'

'Your list of the common extent of accomplishments,' said Darcy, 'has too much truth. The word is applied to many a woman who deserves it no otherwise than by netting a purse or covering a screen. But I am very far from agreeing with you in your estimation of ladies in general. I cannot boast of knowing more than half a dozen, in the whole range of my acquaintance, that are really accomplished.'"

⬦ *Mansfield Park*

"He did not want abilities but he had no curiosity, and no information beyond his profession; he read only the newspaper and the navy-list; he talked only of the dockyard, the harbour, Spithead, and the Motherbank; he swore and he drank, he was dirty and gross."

"Fanny read to herself that 'it was with infinite concern the newspaper had to announce to the world a matrimonial *fracas* in the family of Mr. R. of Wimpole Street; the beautiful Mrs. R., whose name had not long been enrolled in the lists of Hymen, and who had promised to become so brilliant a leader in the fashionable world, having quitted her husband's roof in company with the well-known and captivating Mr. C., the intimate friend and associate of Mr. R., and it was not known even to the editor of the newspaper whither they were gone.'"

❖ Emma

"Emma has been meaning to read more ever since she was twelve years old. I have seen a great many lists of her drawing up at various times of books that she meant to read regularly through—and very good lists they were—very well chosen, and very neatly arranged—sometimes alphabetically, and sometimes by some other rule. The list she drew up when only fourteen—I remember thinking it did her judgment so much credit, that I preserved it some time; and I dare say she may have made out a very good list now."

❖ Persuasion

"When she could let her attention take its natural course again, she found the Miss Musgroves just fetching the Navy List (their own navy list, the first that had ever been at Uppercross), and sitting down together to pore over it, with the professed view of finding out the ships which Captain Wentworth had commanded."

❖ Northanger Abbey

"Dear creature! How much I am obliged to you; and when you have finished Udolpho, we will read the Italian together; and I have made out a list of ten or twelve more of the same kind for you."

"Have you, indeed! How glad I am! What are they all?"

"I will read you their names directly; here they are, in my pocketbook. Castle of Wolfenbach, Clermont, Mysterious Warnings, Necromancer of the Black Forest, Midnight Bell, Orphan of the Rhine, and Horrid Mysteries. Those will last us some time."

"Yes, pretty well; but are they all horrid, are you sure they are all horrid?"

Bonus List: Jane's Royal Ancestors

Jane Austen's family tree courtesy of Ron Dunning,
www.janeaustensfamily.co.uk

SHAKESPEAREAN ANCESTORS

- *Richard II*
  - Earl of Northumberland, tenth great-grandfather
  - Henry "Hotspur" Percy and Lady Percy, eleventh great-grandparents
  - John of Gaunt, twelfth great-grandfather
  - Edmund of Langley, thirteenth great-uncle
  - Lord Berkeley, first cousin, thirteen times removed
- *Henry IV pt 1*
  - Owen Glendower (Owain Glyndwr), thirteenth great-grandfather
  - Hotspur and Lady Percy
- *Macbeth*
  - King Duncan I of Scotland, twenty-first great-grandfather

ROYAL ANCESTORS

- John of Gaunt (twelfth great-grandfather, above) was the son of King Edward III. Thus he and therefore Jane Austen were descended from most previous English kings.
- William the Conqueror, twentieth great-grandfather
- Henry I, nineteenth great-grandfather
- Empress Matilda, eighteenth great-grandmother
- Henry II and Elinor of Aquitaine, seventeenth great-grandparents
- John "Lackland" (the evil King John of Robin Hood), sixteenth great-grandfather
- Henry III, fifteenth great-grandfather
- Edwards I and II, fourteenth great-grandfathers*
- Edward III, thirteenth great-grandfather
- John of Gaunt, twelfth great grandfather

FRENCH ROYALTY

- Robert II, King of France, twenty-first great-grandfather
- (Possibly others)

*Edwards I and II are joint fourteenth great-grandfathers because Edward I's son, and Edward II's brother, Edmund of Woodstock, was a thirteenth great-grandfather of Jane's through his own descendants.

ROYAL RELATIVES

- Mary, Queen of Scots, fourth cousin, seven times removed
- Henry VIII, second cousin, nine times removed
- Queen Elizabeth I, third cousin, eight times removed

OTHER RELATIVES

- William IX, Duke of Aquitaine, best known today as the earliest troubadour, a vernacular lyric poet in the Occitan language, whose work has survived, nineteenth great-grandfather

- Elizabeth (Bess) Throckmorton, third cousin, seven times removed
  - Bess was the wife of Sir Walter Raleigh and a Lady of the Privy Chamber to Queen Elizabeth I of England. They married without the permission of the Queen, whose ladies were expected to gain her permission, which resulted in a long period of royal disfavor for Raleigh.

- Faith Coghill, first cousin, twice removed
  - The wife of Sir Christopher Wren

Bibliography

DEIRDRE LE FAYE: FORTY YEARS OF AUSTEN SCHOLARSHIP

BOOKS

- *Reminiscences of Caroline Austen*
- *Jane Austen: A Family Record*
- *The Jane Austen Cookbook*
- *Jane Austen's Letters,* Third Edition
- *Jane Austen's Letters,* Fourth Edition
- *Writers' Lives: Jane Austen*
- *Fanny Knight's Diaries: Jane Austen through Her Niece's Eyes*
- *Jane Austen's "Outlandish Cousin": The Life and Letters of Eliza de Feuillide*
- *So You Think You Know Jane Austen?*
- *A Chronology of Jane Austen and Her Family, 1600–2000*
- *Jane Austen's Steventon*

PAPERS AND ARTICLES

"Jane Austen and Her Hancock Relatives"

"Hancock Family Grave"

"What Was the History of Fanny Price's Mother?"

"'The Business of Mothering': Two Austenian Dialogues"

"The Nephew Who Missed Jane Austen"

"Recollections of Chawton"

"Tom Lefroy and Jane Austen"

"Fanny Knight"

"Three Austen Family Letters"

"Jane Austen and Mrs. Hunter's Novel"

"Journey, Waterparties and Plays"

"'Sanditon': Jane Austen's MS and Her Niece's Continuation"

"Jane Austen Verses"

"Jane Austen and William Haley"

"News from Chawton: A Letter from Mrs. George Austen"

"The Austens and the Littleworths"

"Jane Austen: Some Letters Re-dated"

"Jane Austen's Verses and Lord Stanhope's Disappointment"

"Anna Lefroy's Original Memories of Jane Austen"

"To Dwell Together in Unity"

"A Jane Austen Manuscript"

"Jane Austen's Nephew: A Re-identification"

"Jane Austen: More Letters Re-dated"

"James Austen's Poetical Biography of John Bond"

"Jane Austen: New Biographical Comments"

"The History of England, by Jane Austen"

"James Austen, Army Chaplain"

"A Literary Portrait Re-examined: Jane Austen and Mary Anne Campion"

"Mrs. George Austen's Will"

"The Devonshire Roots of *Sense and Sensibility*"

"The Geographical Settings of *Pride and Prejudice*"

"Chronology of Jane Austen's Life"

"Jane Austen and the Rice Portrait"

"'A Persecuted Relation': Mrs. Lillingston's Funeral and Jane Austen's Legacy"

"Zincke Miniature Purchased for the Society"

"Silhouettes of the Revd. William Knight and His Family"

"Leonora Austen"

"*Northanger Abbey* and Mrs. Allen's Maxims"

"Jane Austen and the 'Kalendar of Flora': Verses Identified"

"Jane Austen's Friend Mrs. Barrett Identified"

"Three Missing Jane Austen Songs"

"Jane Austen's Friends at Canterbury Cathedral"

"Mr. Austen's Insurance Policy"

"Another Book Owned by Mr. Austen"

"Which Jane Austen Stitched This Sampler?"

"New Marginalia in Jane Austen's Books"

"Jane Austen's Laggard Suitor"

"The Lime Tree at Steventon Rectory"

"The Ball at Basingstoke"

"Lord Brabourne's Edition of Jane Austen's Letters"

"New Introduction to Jane Austen's Letters"

"Anna Lefroy and Her Austen Family Letters"

"Another Piece of Missing Lace"

"'Chronology,' 'Letters,' 'Memoirs and Biographies' in Jane Austen in Context"

"The Austens and Their Wedgwood Ware"

"A Tour of Carlton House"

"More Austen Family Verses"

"Son of Melesina: Charles Manners St. George (1787–1864)"

"Jane Austen in Gloucestershire"

"Lyme Regis Before and After Jane Austen"

"Jane Austen in the 1890s"

"Jane Austen, Her Biographies and Biographers; or, 'Conversations Minutely Repeated'"

"Imaginary Portraits of Jane Austen"

"By Rail and Road: Touring in the North of England in 1837"

"'There cannot be a more worthy young man': Revd. Edward Cooper (1770–1833)"

"The Cult of Jane Austen: 'Her Fame is Far from Universal'"

"The Memoir of Jane Austen and the Cheney Brothers"

"Jane Austen and Bristol"

"Austen Papers 1704–1856: An Updating"

"Catherine Hubback's Memoir of Francis Austen"

"Jane Austen and the Miss Curlings"

"Jane Austen's Smack"

"Three Telltale Words; or, Not Jane Austen's Portrait"

BOOKS

Auerbach, Emily. *Searching for Jane Austen*. Madison, Wis.: University of Wisconsin Press, 2004.

Austen, Caroline. *My Aunt Jane Austen: A Memoir*. Edited by R. W. Chapman. Winchester, UK: Jane Austen Society, 1991.

Austen, Jane. *Sense and Sensibility*. Edited by R. W. Chapman. 3rd ed. London: Oxford University Press, 1988.

———. *Pride and Prejudice*. Edited by R. W. Chapman. 3rd ed. London: Oxford University Press, 1988.

————. *Mansfield Park*. Edited by R. W. Chapman. 3rd ed. London: Oxford University Press, 1988.

————. *Emma*. Edited by R. W. Chapman. 3rd ed. London: Oxford University Press, 1988.

————. *Northanger Abbey*. Edited by R. W. Chapman. 3rd ed. London: Oxford University Press, 1988.

————. *Persuasion*. Edited by R. W. Chapman. 3rd ed. London: Oxford University Press, 1988.

————. *Minor Works*. Edited by R. W. Chapman. 1st ed. London: Oxford University Press, 1988.

Austen-Leigh, James Edward. *A Memoir of Jane Austen*. London: Folio Society, 1989. (First published in 1870)

Austen-Leigh, William and Richard Arthur Austen-Leigh. *Jane Austen: Her Life and Letters: A Family Record*. New York: Barnes and Noble, 2006. (First published in 1913)

Baker, William. *A Critical Companion to Jane Austen: A Literary Reference to Her Life and Work*. New York: Facts on File, 2008.

Byrde, Penelope. *Jane Austen Fashion: Fashion and Needlework in the Works of Jane Austen*. Ludlow, Shropshire, UK: Excellent Press, 2008.

Collins, Irene. *Jane Austen and the Clergy*. Rio Grande, OH: Hambledon Press, 1993.

————. *Jane Austen: The Parson's Daughter*. Rio Grande, OH: Hambledon Press, 1998.

Edwards, Anne-Marie. *In the Steps of Jane Austen*. Madison, WI: Jones Books, 2003.

Fullerton, Susannah. *A Dance with Jane Austen: How a Novelist and Her Characters Went to the Ball*. London: Frances Lincoln, 2012.

————. *Jane Austen and Crime*. Madison, WI: Jones Books, 2006.

Gammie, Ian and Derek McCulloch. *Jane Austen's Music*. Saint Albans, UK: Corda Music, 1996.

Gilson, David. *A Bibliography of Jane Austen*. New Castle, DE: Oak Knoll Press, 1997.

Hill, Constance. *Jane Austen: Her Homes and Her Friends*. London: John Lane, 1902.

Honan, Park. *Jane Austen: Her Life*. New York: St. Martin's Press, 1988.

Jones, Vivien, ed. *Jane Austen: Selected Letters*. Oxford, UK: Oxford University Press, 2004.

Lane, Maggie. *A Charming Place: Bath in the Life and Times of Jane Austen.* Bath, UK: Millstream Books, 1988.

Le Faye, Deirdre. *A Chronology of Jane Austen and Her Family, 1600–2000.* Cambridge: Cambridge University Press, 2006.

———, ed. *Fanny Knight's Diaries: Jane Austen through Her Niece's Eyes.* Winchester, UK: Jane Austen Society, 2000.

———. *Jane Austen: A Family Record.* 2nd ed. Cambridge: Cambridge University Press, 2004.

———, ed. *Jane Austen's Letters.* 3rd ed. Oxford: Oxford University Press, 1995.

———, ed. *Jane Austen's Letters.* 4th ed. Oxford: Oxford University Press, 2011.

———, ed. *Reminiscences of Jane Austen's Niece Caroline Austen.* Winchester, UK: Jane Austen Society, 2004.

McMaster, Juliet, ed. *Three Mini-Dramas by Jane Austen.* Sydney, Australia: Juvenilia Press, 2006.

Modert, Jo, ed. *Jane Austen's Manuscript Letters in Facsimile: Reproductions of Every Known Extant Letter, Fragment, and Autograph Copy, with an Annotated List of All Known Letters.* Carbondale, IL: Southern Illinois University Press, 1990.

Nokes, David. *Jane Austen: A Life.* New York: Farrar, Straus & Giroux, 1997.

Olsen, Kirstin. *All Things Austen: An Encyclopedia of Jane Austen's World.* Westport, CT: Greenwood Press, 2005.

Poplawski, Paul. *A Jane Austen Encyclopedia.* Westport, CT: Greenwood Press, 1998.

Ray, Joan Klingel. *Jane Austen for Dummies.* Hoboken, NJ: Wiley, 2006.

Selwyn, David, ed. *The Poetry of Jane Austen and the Austen Family.* Iowa City: University of Iowa Press, 1997.

Southam, B. C. *Jane Austen: The Critical Heritage*, vol. 1, *1811–1879.* New York: Taylor and Francis, 2007.

Spence, Jon. *Becoming Jane Austen.* New York: Hambledon Continuum, 2007.

Tomalin, Claire. *Jane Austen: A Life.* New York: Vintage Books, 1999.

Tyler, Natalie. *The Friendly Jane Austen: A Well-mannered Introduction to a Lady of Sense and Sensibility.* New York: Viking, 1999.

Upfal, Annette and Christine Alexander, ed. *Jane Austen's* The History of England. Sydney, Australia: Juvenilia Press, 2009.

———. *Jane Austen's* Lady Susan. Sydney, Australia: Juvenilia Press, 2005.

Watkins, Susan. *Jane Austen's Town and Country Style*. New York: Rizzoli International Publications, 1990.

Wilson, Kim. *In the Garden with Jane Austen*. Madison, WI: Jones Books, 2008.

———. *Tea with Jane Austen*. Madison, WI: Jones Books, 2004.

JOURNALS AND PUBLICATIONS

Jane Austen's Regency World. Bath, UK.

Persuasions: The Jane Austen Journal. Journal of the Jane Austen Society of North America.

OTHER SOURCES

Brooks, Jeanine, Professor of Music, University of Southampton, UK.

LIBRARIES AND MUSEUMS

British Library

British Museum

Chawton House Library

Hampshire Museums Service

Jane Austen's House Museum

London Library

Madison Public Library

Morgan Library

New York Public Library

University of California Libraries

University of Chicago Library

University of Wisconsin Libraries

Jane Austen Societies

Jane Austen Society of North America: www.jasna.org

Jane Austen Society: www.janeaustensoci.freeuk.com

Jane Austen Society of Australia: www.jasa.net.au

Websites

Archives of the Austen-L listserv, mcgill.ca

austenblog.com

austenonly.com

austenprose.com

gutenberg.org

janeausteninvermont.wordpress.com

janeaustensfamily.co.uk

janeaustensworld.wordpress.com

janitesonthejames.blogspot.com

Jane Austen's Fiction Manuscripts Digital Edition: janeausten.ac.uk

mollands.net

onelondonone.blogspot.com

pemberley.com

reveriesunderthesignofausten.wordpress.com

rootsweb.ancestory.com

sharpelvessociety.blogspot.com

The List Lover's Guide to the Author

JOAN STRASBAUGH

- Publishing professional
- Organized the Jane Austen in the 21st Century Humanities Festival at the University of Wisconsin
- Janeite since 2001
- Author of two books
- Lives in New York, New York